SKETCHED FOR THE SAKE OF THE REMEMBRA

a visual diary of Louisa Paris' English travels 1852-54

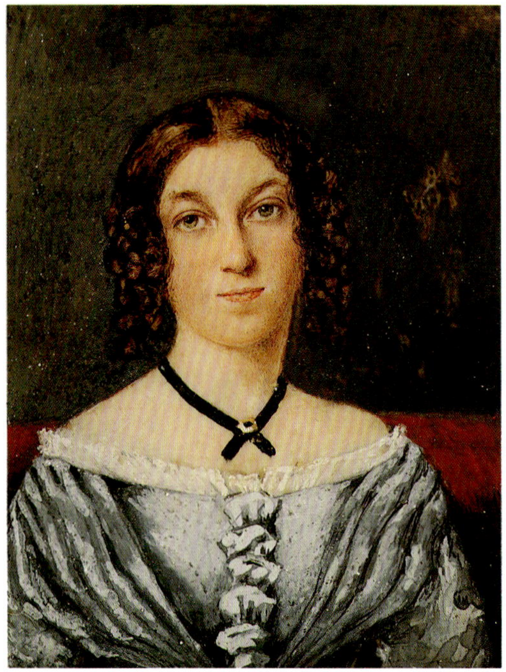

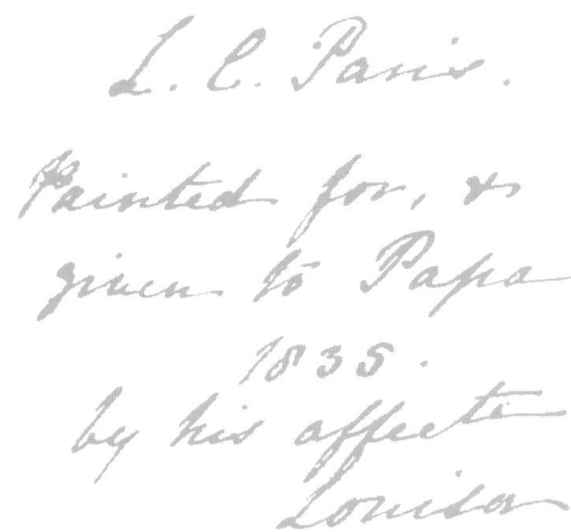

3 *Self Portrait (?)* 1835
Oil on ivory (reproduced actual size)
Inscribed on reverse:
L.C.Paris.
Painted for, & given to Papa 1835.
by his affect(ionate) Louisa.
Private Collection.

SKETCHED FOR THE SAKE OF THE REMEMBRANCE

a visual diary of Louisa Paris' English travels 1852-54

TOWNER
ART GALLERY
& LOCAL MUSEUM
EASTBOURNE

Catalogue produced in association with the exhibition
SKETCHED FOR THE SAKE OF THE REMEMBRANCE
a visual diary of Louisa Paris' English travels 1852-54
15th July - 17th September 1995
Exhibition organised by Penny Johnson
Towner Art Gallery & Local Museum, Eastbourne

Sponsored by

CFM Group Ltd is an award winner under the National Heritage Arts Sponsorship Scheme for its support of the Towner Art Gallery & Local Museum's exhibition
SKETCHED FOR THE SAKE OF THE REMEMBRANCE
a visual diary of Louisa Paris' English travels 1852-54
The 'Pairing Scheme' is a Government Scheme administered by ABSA (Association for Business Sponsorship of the Arts)

ISBN No: 1 871360 07 2
Catalogue designed by Jeremy Brook, Graphic Ideas, Hastings
Printed by Weald Press, St Leonards on Sea
Photographs by Jerry Bird, Stephen Curtis and John Gascoigne

Front Cover
Detail of **35** *The old town of Eastbourne in the valley, taken from the top of the Downs. F, R, E and myself spent the day on the Downs. 4th Sept. 1852 taken from the Links Down.*

Contents

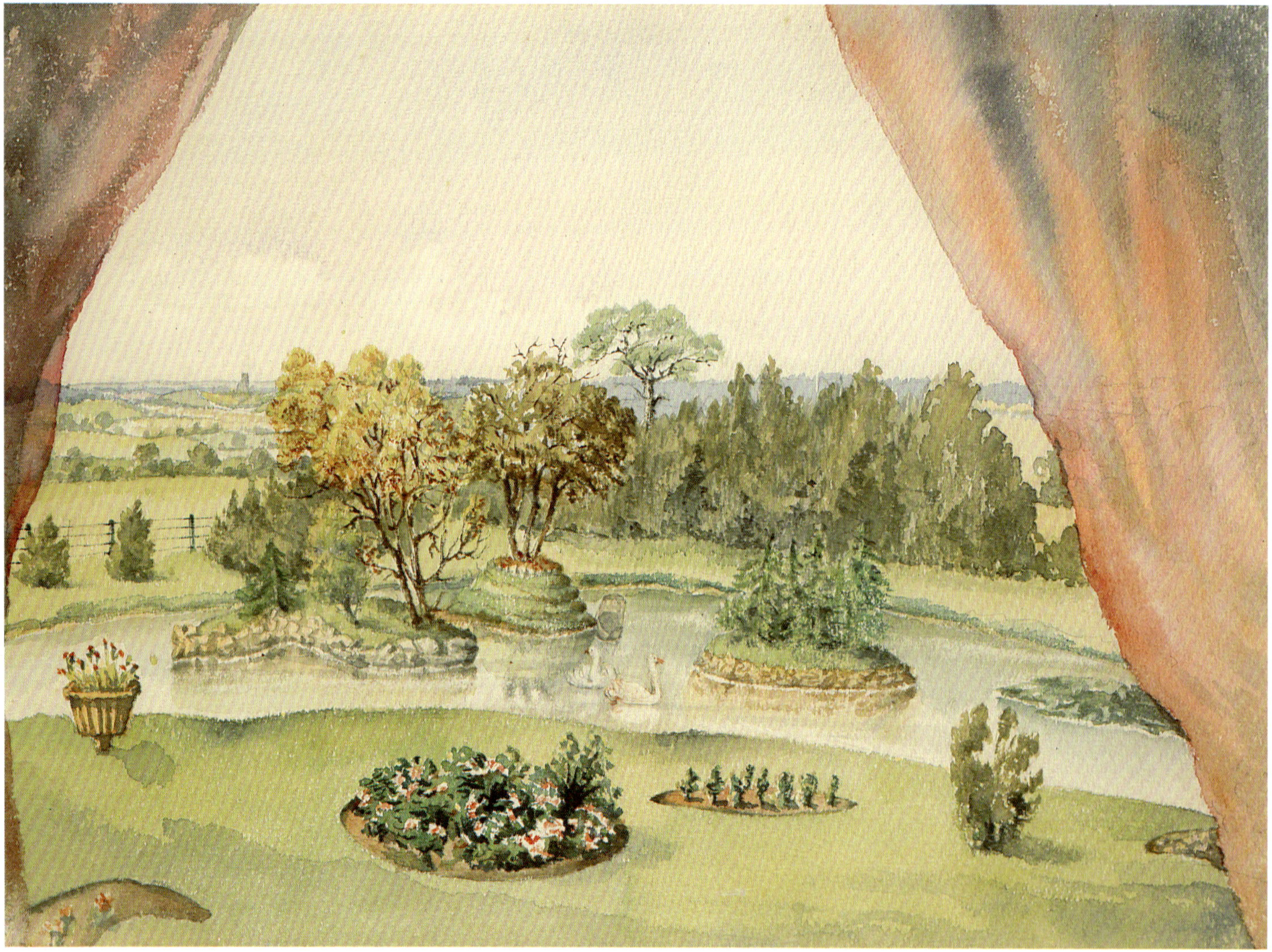

7 *View from my bedroom, Cockfield, got up very early and sketched before breakfast. 1852. Louisa C Paris –*

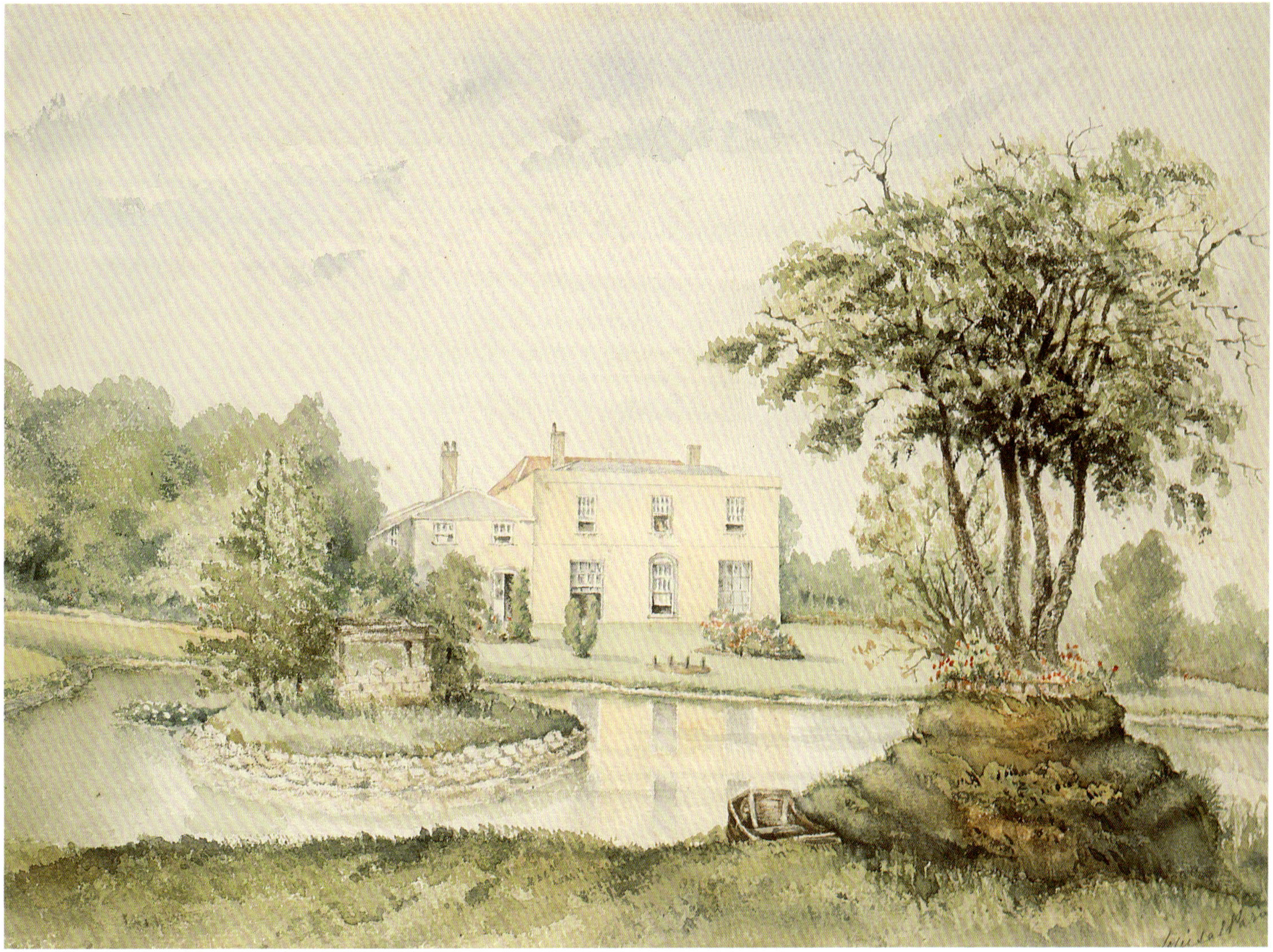

9 *Back of Rectory, Cockfield, sat out under the trees sketching with Mrs. Watson – 'till luncheon, driven in by a violent thunder-storm. very warm day! June 1852.*

Foreword

I have been intrigued by Louisa Paris since I arrived at the Towner Art Gallery and Local Museum in 1987. Here was a collection of 78 watercolours painted between 1852 and 1854 by an accomplished and witty amateur artist. They depict views and places in South East England, including 22 of Eastbourne. They are atmospheric interpretations of place as well as having historical value in recording a changing landscape. What takes these beyond the usual topographical views is that the artist has written lively captions underneath each picture, giving account of the circumstances in which they were painted. Through this combination not only can we delight in the charm of her visual descriptions but also gain insight into her personal life. A day sketching at Pevensey Castle ended in near calamity when it was discovered that they had no transport home:

> *"...our conveyance had disappeared! that there was not another to be had in the neighbourhood, not even a cart!! and the last train departed, before we discovered our melancholy situation! at last, at 1/2 past 8 a fly appeared!! our dinner having been ordered at six!! Augst 23rd 1852"*

Who was Louisa Paris? What was her family situation and who were Rosa, Ellen and Muff?

When the watercolours were acquired by the Towner in 1960, it was suggested that Louisa Paris was the daughter of a London surgeon. Twenty years later Dr. Patricia Andrew, the then Deputy Director of the Towner, began research which unearthed a considerable amount about Louisa Paris' family, the landscapes and architecture depicted in the paintings and the fact that she died in 1875. But details about Louisa Paris were tantalisingly few. My curiosity was stirred. Rather like a detective, the proven facts were examined for the next lead: Louisa Paris had died in a lunatic asylum at Laverstock near Salisbury. Their register revealed that she had lived on the Isle of Wight before her admission. This proved to be an extremely valuable fact. We placed a letter in the island's main journal asking for information on the artist. This led to a reader contacting a friend in Australia, who in turn contacted her sister in Shropshire and who then informed us that she was a descendant of Louisa Paris and had some of her work. We couldn't believe our luck. We were to discover a group of pencil sketches executed in 1833, nineteen years earlier than the watercolours in the Towner's Collection. The drawings are remarkable because they document so graphically her development as an artist, from the early copies of other artists' work, towards her own unmistakable style.

This was not enough. We were still trying to find out more about Louisa's life. Happily, a second sketchbook containing drawings and watercolours by Louisa Paris was found, and we also traced two further works, a portrait of her father painted in 1832 and what is thought to be a self portrait of 1835. This was an exciting find as it is the only likeness that has been discovered.

Her date of birth was still a mystery. Parish records in London were checked but to no avail. Eventually through contacting another side of the family we learned that although she was born in London she had not been baptised until two years later while the family were living in Cornwall. Louisa Paris was born on 21st May 1811. Now we know that the watercolours in the Towner Collection are the work of a woman in her early forties, and with the additional new finds we can be sure she began her artistic output by at least the age of twenty. The missing link in the jigsaw is what happened to her work after 1854. Did she suddenly stop? Did something happen to her? Will a collection of sketches produced after 1854 turn up in someone's attic? We would still like to know more about her circumstances.

In spite of her self-effacing style and comments she is none the less a strong presence in the pictures. Look out for little reminders, like her painting equipment scattered in the foreground. I do hope you will enjoy the exhibition as much as we have putting it together.

Penny Johnson
Curator

Throughout the catalogue the captions inscribed by Louisa Paris below the watercolours are in italics and maintain her original spelling and punctuation. The bracketed numbers in bold in the essays refer to the catalogue numbers of the watercolours, which are listed at the end of this publication.

Acknowledgements

I am very pleased that this exhibition presents the newly discovered drawings, watercolours and portraits alongside the Towner's own collection of watercolours. In order to be able to do this, we have received the help of many people. I am particularly grateful to Sue Thomas for her commitment and tireless research and for her biographical essay in this catalogue. I was delighted when Frances Borzello, the art historian, on being introduced to the watercolours also became intrigued, and agreed to explore the social context in which Louisa Paris worked. Her insightful account of *Spent the day in sketching: The Life of a Victorian Lady Amateur Artist* is not only fascinating, but it puts Louisa Paris' work into a historical framework.

Sue Thomas and I wish to thank members of Louisa Paris' family who have given us access to their possessions relating to the artist and have kindly lent material to the exhibition. We are indebted to the Editor of the Isle of Wight County Press for carrying our letter of request for information and to those readers who responded so positively. We would also like to thank the staff of the Royal College of Physicians and Salisbury Record Office.

I should like to acknowledge Jerry Bird, Sarah Blessington, Norman Culshaw, Joanne Dobson, Mary Elliott, Kate Fowle, Colin Napier, Anne Russell and Catherine Tonge, the Towner staff, who have all contributed in different ways to the preparation of the exhibition.

Finally, it would not have been possible to publish the new information about Louisa Paris in a catalogue with colour illustrations without the generous sponsorship of CFM Group Ltd. I much appreciated the enthusiasm with which Dr Vince Padi, the Marketing Manager of CFM, greeted the project and thank him, his colleague Phil Gardner and Allen Gales, the Borough Treasurer of Eastbourne Borough Council for their support and help in realising the sponsorship. As a result of the sponsorship CFM Group Ltd is an award winner under the *Pairing Scheme,* (the National Heritage Arts Sponsorship Scheme) for its support of the Towner Art Gallery & Local Museum.

Penny Johnson

Curator

Louisa Catherine Paris 1811-1875

Louisa was the eldest child of Mary Catherine and Dr. John Ayrton Paris (1785-1856.) Dr. Paris was an eminent physician, whose life and work is documented, somewhat inaccurately, in the *Dictionary of National Biography*. He was born in Cambridge, educated at Fairton Grammer School and entered Caius College, Cambridge in 1803. According to the *Dictionary*: "His means were small and on 3rd January 1804 he was appointed to one of the studentships in physic founded for poor students by Squire Tancred." In spite of this, his family had literary connections and his mother, Elizabeth Ayrton Paris, was a friend of Charles and Mary Lamb. Dr. Paris graduated from Caius in 1808, and came to London where he gained the patronage of Dr. William George Maton, a physician at Westminster Hospital. In 1809, aged 28, he succeeded Dr. Maton on his retirement and married Mary Catherine Noble, daughter of Francis Noble of Fordham Abbey, Cambridge in the same year. Louisa was born on May 21st 1811. The couple continued to live in London until 1813, the year Dr. Paris became a Doctor of Medicine. Here *The Dictionary of National Biography* ceases to be of use in charting the Doctor's family, as it states that he has one son, Thomas Clifton Paris. In fact Dr. Paris had nine children (although only eight are named in his will). In 1813 on the recommendation of Dr. Maton, Dr. Paris accepted a post in Penzance, Cornwall. While living here he became first secretary of the Royal Geological Society of Cornwall. He also invented the Safety-bar, which was a simple instrument designed to prevent the premature explosion of gun powder, and which must have saved the lives of many Cornish miners.

It was in Penzance that Louisa's sister, Fanny, was born on 16th September 1814. In 1817 the family returned to London and took the house at 27 Dover Street *(Fig. 1)*, where they were to live until Dr. Paris' death in 1856. In 1818 Thomas Clifton (Tom) was born, followed by Rosa Caroline in 1819 or 1820, John Rose in 1824 and Charles Bingham in 1825. From the ages given in the 1851 census, it seems likely that Matthew was born around 1826, Jane 1829 and Sarah Eleanor or Ellen 1830. Fortunately, the house in Dover Street was large and remains intact today, looking, at least on the outside, much as it must have looked then.

Although Dr. Paris had a large family to support, his income from medical practice and lecturing must have enabled him to provide the fashionable trappings of Victorian middle class life and ensure his

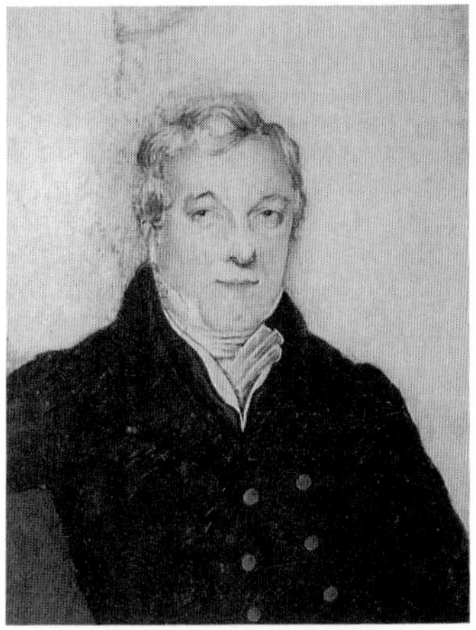

1 *Portrait of Dr. John Ayrton Paris 1832*

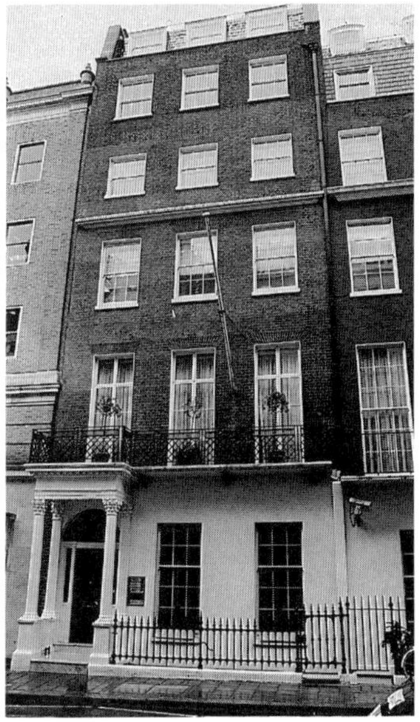

Fig. 1 The house at 27 Dover Street, London where the Paris Family lived 1817-56? (photo. 1995).

children enjoyed a comfortable and secure youth. A Fellow of the College of Physicians since 1814, Dr. Paris was appointed its President in 1844, a position he retained until his death. His diverse interests, conversational powers and fondness of anecdotes made him popular in society though much of his time was devoted to chemistry, keeping pace with rapid advances. He also wrote several books published between 1812 and 1831 (see *Publications by Dr. Paris* at the end of this essay). One of these, *Philosophy in Sport Made Science in Earnest*, published in 1827 with illustrations by George Cruikshank, is of particular interest because of the autobiographical aspect. Dr. Paris writes under the name Seymour and explains in the Foreword that it was originally composed for the exclusive use of his children in order to teach them scientific principles through the use of toys and games.

Louisa, Tom, Fanny, Rosa and John all feature in the book through lessons linked with a storyline based around events in the family house, 'Overton Lodge', and in the village of Overton. This suggests that the Paris family had a country home in addition to the Dover Street house (possibly the 'Over Staploe' mentioned later in Louisa's will.) Tom, who is home on holiday from school, is the main recipient of the lessons. Louisa too, features prominently in the book:

> "I trust that Louisa and Fanny, who are of an age to understand the subject, will not prove uninterested spectators. Little John, too, will profit by our scheme, for as I shall necessarily require, for illustration, certain toys which can scarcely afford any amusement to a boy of your age and acquirements, it is but fair that they should be transferred into his hands." (Vol. 1 page 21)

Louisa's interest in music is commented on in the book but there is no mention of drawing or painting.

It would seem that these latter pursuits did not feature so strongly in Louisa's life at this stage, aged 16. Her earliest known picture is a portrait of her father painted in February 1832 (**1**) when she was nearly 21. This shows a delicate but confident handling of the facial features and suggestion of character. In the sketchbook of a year later, her development in draughtmanship is clearly demonstrated (**2**). The first few pages contain drawings copied from other sources, while the later drawings give her own interpretation of a scene with captions. The green leather bound sketchbook with portraits in pencil and watercolour, dating from 1837-1849, has a charming frontispiece with Louisa's name hand-painted in a pink, yellow, purple and green floral arrangement (4). Louisa's increasing accomplishment in watercolour is evident in the series of views of South East England completed between 1852 and 1854. Her visits incorporated Cockfield in Suffolk and Eastbourne in 1852 and Penshurst and Broadstairs in Kent in 1853. By this time sketching held a central role in her daily life as indicated in the captions below her paintings: *"sketched after the dew began to fall"* and *"got up very early and sketched before breakfast"*. She also mentions her sketching and travelling companions, members of her family or friends she is staying with, and their daily excursions. She visited Cockfield on several occasions, staying at Cockfield Rectory with the Watsons, who are assumed to be friends. There are, however, no Watsons recorded in the locality at this date, so the family were also probably visitors to the village. In October 1854 Louisa and members of her family, including Muff the dog, stayed at Saltwood, Kent on what may have been the last family holiday as her mother died in June 1855.

The death of Mrs Paris marked the beginning of a change in circumstances for the family. From Louisa's captions it seems that she was close to her mother and she must have felt her loss keenly. A further tragedy occured only a little more than a year later when Dr. Paris also died at their home in Dover Street, on 4th December 1856, of a "malignant disease of the bladder". In his will he left instructions to sell the house and divide the estate. The share of his daughters being held in trust (at least as far as can be deciphered from the will). He names his sons Thomas Clifton and John Rose as executors. As there is no documented evidence it is only possible to speculate as to what happened to the family after the death of both parents.

It is known that Jane married at some point, and may have already left home by 1856. Charles Bingham had long gone to Liverpool to pursue his career and raise a family (he also became Honorary Secretary of the St John Ambulance Association) and Thomas and John both had careers. John was a clerk in the Admirality from 1845-66 and Naval Storekeeper from 1866-70. Tom, having been educated at

Harrow and Trinity College, Cambridge, had become a barrister in 1842. Of Matthew nothing is known. By 1861 the census for Dover Street gives a different family living at number 27. The children of Dr. Paris must have gone their separate ways after his death.

Later in 1858, Dr. Paris' daughters were awarded a pension from the Queen. The letter from Lord Palmerston which communicated this information acknowledged Dr. Paris' literary and philosophical attainments and comments on the great expenses incurred in maintaining a large family.

> "It is with much satisfaction we are able to state that Her Majesty has granted a pension of £150 per annum to the daughters of the late Dr. Paris. This gracious act of the Sovereign was communicated to the Misses Paris by a letter from Lord Palmerston forwarded to them through Sir Henry Holland. This honourable testimony to the work of Dr. Paris cannot fail to be gratifying to all, especially to men of science and to the medical profession..." *The Lancet*, January 9th 1858.

The only member of her family traceable during the 1860s is Tom. An obiturary from the *Hereford Times* on January 30th 1909 has the following information: "from 1858 to 1872 he was engaged in the literary department of the principal registry at Somerset House, and on May 31st 1872, was appointed Registrar of Hereford Court, a post which he held until his death" on 26th January 1909. The newspaper also stated:

> "Mr Paris who was a bachelor resided of late years at Hampton Lodge. His principal recreations were hunting and hill climbing. He was the author in 1843 of *Letters from the Pyrenees* and in 1871 of *A Handbook for Travellers in Switzerland and the Alps of Savoy and Piedmont*. Mr Paris was an extremely gifted artist in both oil and watercolour and had exhibited several pictures in the Royal Academy. He was laid to rest in Tupsley Churchyard yesterday."

John lived and died unmarried in Dorset, while Fanny moved to the Isle of Wight at some point and died there aged 101 in Yarmouth. Rosa died unmarried at Brockenhurst in 1889, the 1871 census showing that Ellen lived with her. But of Louisa there is no trace until 1866, when she made a will while living at

Freshwater on the Isle of Wight. However, an earlier directory for Freshwater, Isle of Wight, lists "the Misses Paris" for 1859. She bequeathed her share of the estate, which belonged to her father, 'Over Staploe', to her sisters Fanny, Rosa Caroline and Sarah Eleanor (Ellen) to be divided equally between them, and her personal estate to Rosa and Sarah Eleanor.

It is not known exactly when Louisa came to live on the Isle of Wight but there is evidence that she lived at a property called 'Stoneywynde' at Freshwater, in the same district as the home of Alfred Lord Tennyson, the Poet Laureate. The next factual piece of evidence relating to her is to be found in the register of Laverstock Mental Asylum, near Salisbury where Louisa was commited as a patient in February 1868. The register states that she was sent to the asylum, a "fair accommodation for patients of the middle classes", by her brother Matthew on 8th February 1868. The census for 1871 taken at Laverstock lists Louisa Catherine Paris as an unmarried lunatic patient aged 58 years. She died on 26th November 1875 from "exhaustion from abscess and cancer", a tragic and unexpected end for the woman who had produced such carefree, informal and lively watercolour sketches.

Sue Thomas

Publications by Dr. Paris

Pharmacologia – A General Treatise on Materia Medica and Therapeutics 1812

A Guide to Mount's Bay and Land's End 1815

A Memoir of the Life and Scientific Labours of the Rev. William Gregor 1817

Medical Jurisprudence 1823

The Elements of Medical Chemistry 1825

Philosophy in Sport Made Science in Earnest 1827

A Treatise on Diet 1827

The Life of Sir Humphry Davy 1831

The Paris Family

Dr. John Ayrton Paris (1785-1856)
m.
Mary Catherine Paris (Noble) (1788?-1855)

- **Louisa Catherine Paris** (1811-1875)
- **Fanny Cresswell Paris** (1814-1916)
- **Thomas Clifton Paris** (1818-1909)
- **Rosa Caroline Paris** (1820?-1889)
- **Jane Gregor Paris** (1823-1881)
- **John Rose Paris** (1824-1907)
- **Charles Bingham Paris** (1825-1888)
- **Matthew Paris** (1826?-?)
- **Sarah Eleanor Paris** (1830?-?)

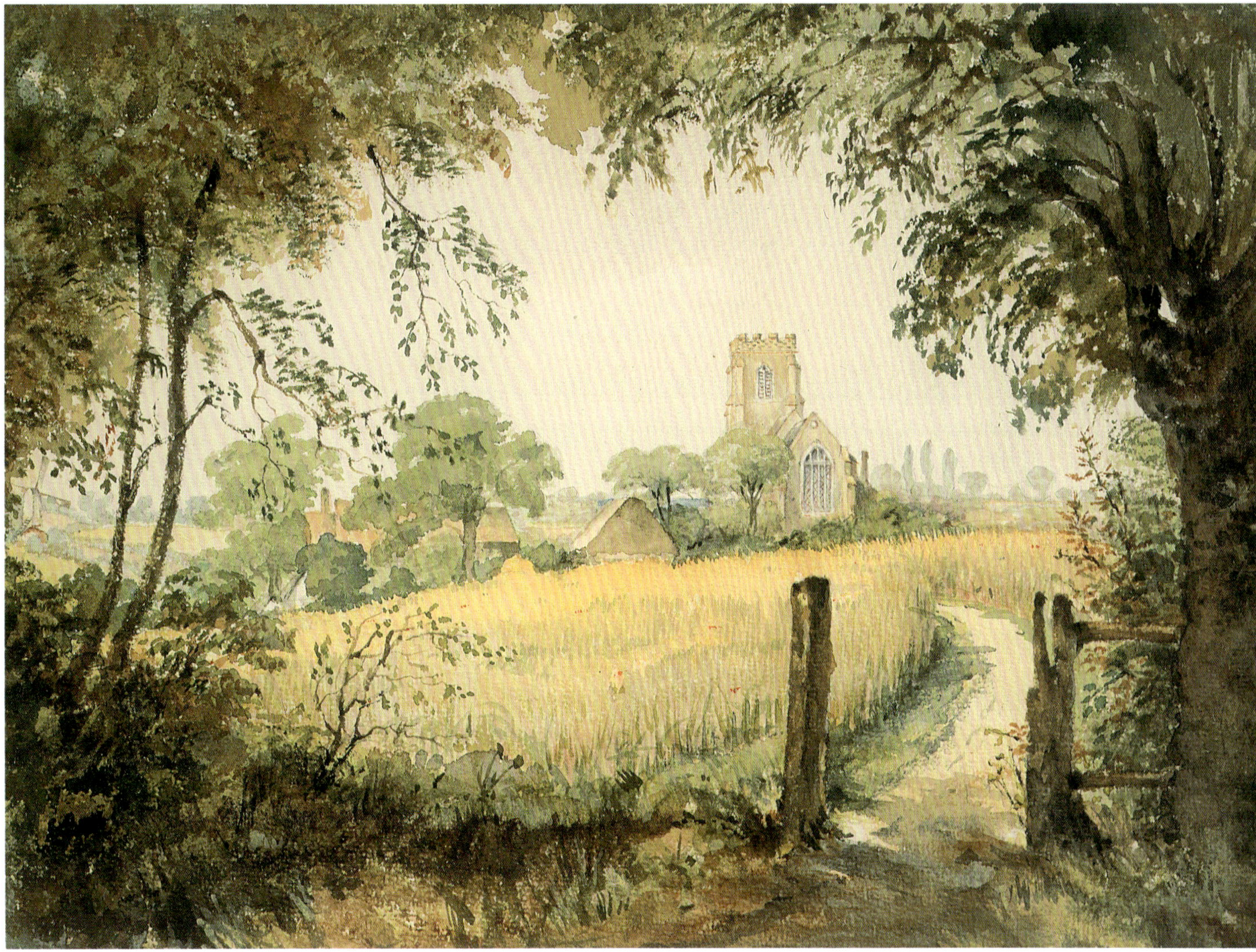

11 *Cockfield Church from one of the fields in the walk to church from the Rectory, July 1852. Louisa C Paris.*

Spent the day in sketching: The Life of a Victorian Lady Amateur Artist

Louisa Paris is an enigma. On the one hand there are the paintings and on the other are the sparse biographical facts and in the middle is a blank. On the surface, nothing could seem more conventional than an unmarried Victorian gentlewoman in her forties engaging in the genteel practice of watercolour painting in the summer holidays. And yet the amused eye and ear which occasionally surface in odd details of her captions and paintings hint at a quirkiness that lifts her away from the stereotype. And the references to family and friends in her words and pictures suggest a life of fulfilment and small but deeply felt pleasures.

However, in one way at least her watercolours fit the stereotype, for they prove that her parents ensured she was equipped with one of the most important female accomplishments of the period. "The art of painting stands pre-eminent among the elegant accomplishments so requisite to the finished education of an individual of either sex in the present day" wrote an amateur in 1831 in *Remarks Upon Landscape Painting in Watercolours*. Eleven years later, Mrs. Ellis told the readers of *Daughters of England* that "the female character though invested with high intellectual endowments, must ever fail to charm, without at least a taste for music, painting, or poetry". It is likely that Louisa came from a family which prided itself on its artistic talents: her captions suggest that only her mother did not paint, and this may have been due to ill health not lack of ability.

In 1824, when Louisa Paris was 13, Catherine F. Newman's *Practical Hints on Female Education* was published. It included a week of timetables as a guide for the governess. Tuesday's schedule ran:

7-8	*Prayer, and Reading Scriptures, and Explanation*
8-9	*Play, or walking out, Lesson of Italian grammar*
9-10	*Breakfast, verbs, Italian or French repeated*
11-12	*Italian, Reading and Examination thereon*
12-1	*Walking, and Conversation on Light Subjects*

1-2	*English , Reading, Arithmetic and Spelling*
2-3	*Dressing for and Dinner, Anecdotes related*
3-4	*Music practised or Lessons taken*
4-5	*Biographical lesson, and Natural History*
5-6	*Walking or Exercise taken within*
6-7	*Tea, Needle-work while read to*
7-8	*Lessons prepared for the following Day*
8-9	*Prayer, Devotional Reading and going to bed*

Three pm was clearly accomplishment hour, with the 'Lessons taken' referring to drawing. Fortunately for Louisa, her father's book, *Philosophy in Sport Made Science in Earnest*, (see Sue Thomas' essay) suggests that her education contained more sustenance than this thin broth.

The young Louisa Paris was probably taught by a governess: with several children in the family, it would have made economic sense. Boarding schools advertising in *The Times* in the 1820s listed fees between £20 and £30 a year per child, with drawing and music as optional extras at one guinea a term. A governess at a salary of £50 a year, with responsibility for the education of all the girls and the youngest boys until they left for boarding school, was a bargain. Most governesses who advertised in *The Times* in the 1820s offered drawing. If they did not, or if one of the children showed a special talent, a drawing teacher might be employed once or twice a week.

Learning to paint in watercolour involved copying other people's drawings and engravings, mastering perspective, and following one of the several compositional formulae and methods of applying paint offered in the drawing manuals. By the early nineteenth century, manuals with instructions based on the figure had begun to look old fashioned. Louisa was probably more familiar with the newer manuals which used illustrations of scenery to make their points, a reflection of the recent rapid development of British landscape painting.

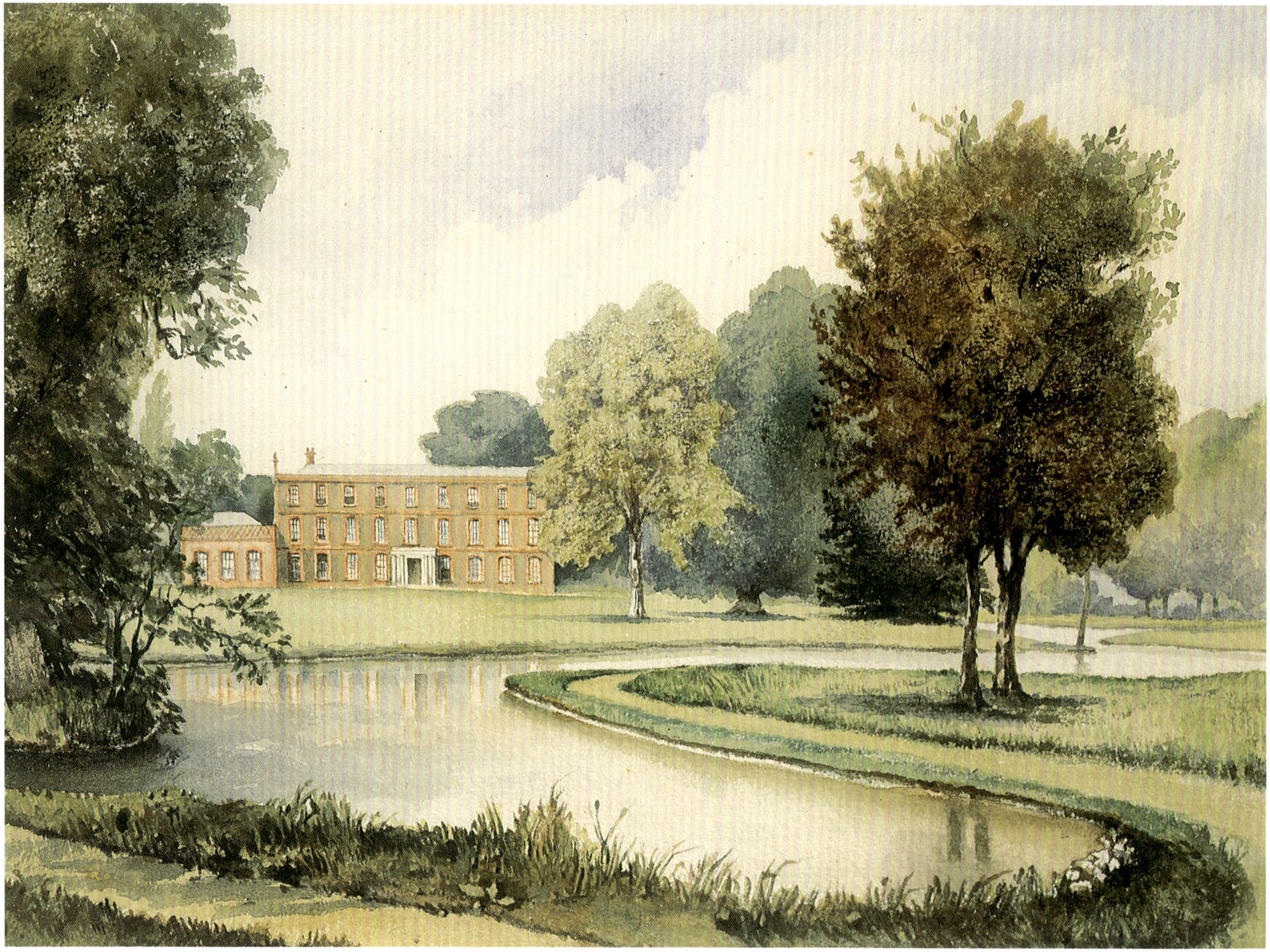

21 *The Hyde, Mr. Disney's, Essex. I spent a very agreeable three days after my visit into Suffolk in 1852. returned to London on the 7th. Aug. afterwards went to Eastbourne to join Mama & the rest of the party.*

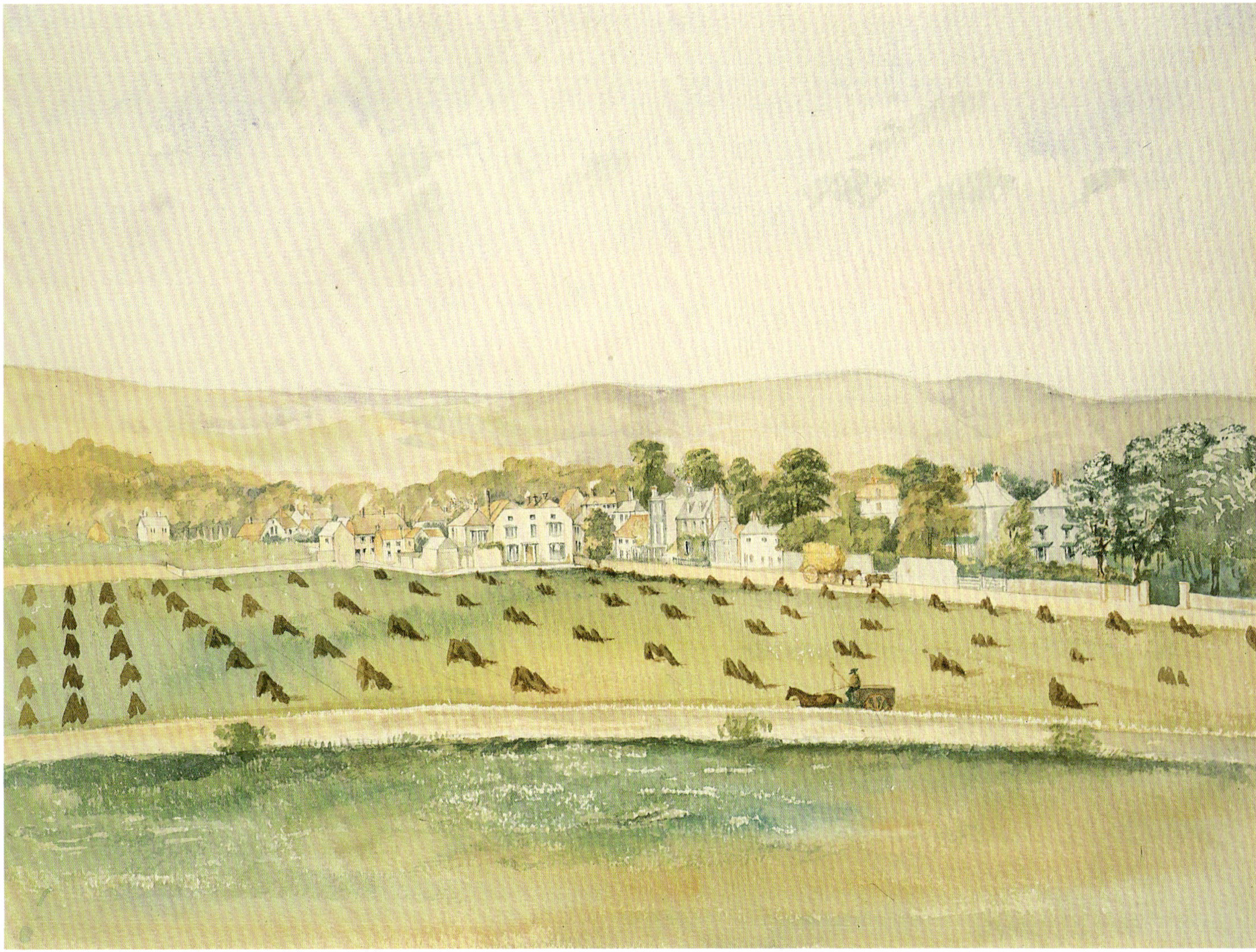

23 *Southbourne, sketched from our staircase window at the back of the house. Eastbourne. August 1852.*

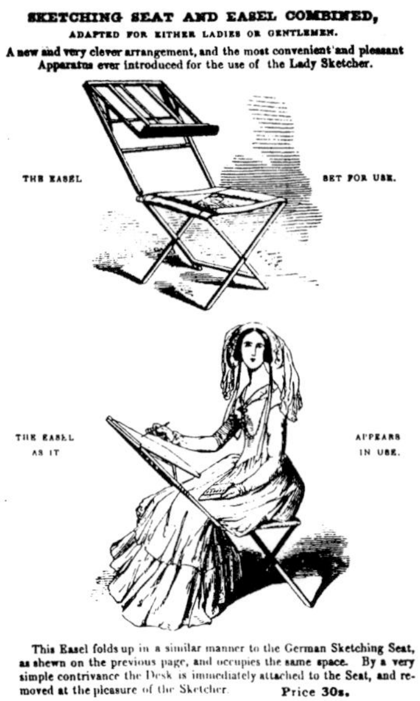

Fig.2 Winsor & Newton catalogue, 1849
Reproduced by courtesy of Winsor & Newton

While all young women learned some drawing in the schoolroom, serious students often continued to take instruction after their studies had officially ended, and there is evidence that Louisa may have been one of them. In *Miniatures, A Dictionary and Guide*, Daphne Foskett records a miniature signed on the reverse "Miss Flipwall/by Louisa Cath. Paris/from Mrs. Greens/April 1833". Given that Louisa signs her middle name in this abbreviated form, it suggests it might indeed be Louisa, aged 24, and Daphne Foskett's guess that Mrs. Green might be Mrs James Green, an artist by then aged 57 who had exhibited widely until 1815 and who took students, is certainly possible. Among the 23 pencil drawings in Louisa's 1833 sketchbook (**2**) are some meticulous drawings of foreign places which are almost certainly copies: their technique is so unlike the other autograph drawings in the sketchbook it suggests that she was following the conventional practice of sharpening her skills by copying the works of others.

There is plenty of evidence from contemporary cartoons, letters, diaries and novels that Louisa Paris was not alone in keeping up her watercolour painting as an adult, although a collection of the Towner Art Gallery's type, size and scope is rare. So substantial was this group of female amateurs that it was targeted by all the major manufacturers of artists' materials in order to increase their sales. Advertisements pitched to appeal to women often featured a product's cleanliness as an important selling point. For example, the advertisement in the June 1842 *Art Union* for a new product called aquaoleum ran as follows: "The dislike that many persons (especially ladies) have to oil colours, on account of their smell, is here entirely avoided, as they have rather a pleasant odour and any stain or soil from them may be removed with water." In 1849, the Winsor and Newton catalogue announced a combined sketching seat and easel as "a new and very clever arrangement and the most convenient and pleasant apparatus ever introduced for the use of the lady sketcher" *(Fig 2)*. Louisa no doubt bought artists' materials, though living in London she could purchase them from shops rather than order by mail. The sketching stool, sketching umbrella, paintbox and palette Louisa puts in her paintings can all be found in contemporary catalogues.

It was possible for an amateur, that is someone who did not earn money from her art, to exhibit. A tantalising reference to a Miss Paris in the Royal Academy exhibition in 1850 may refer to Louisa, especially as a Mr.T.C.Paris also exhibited that year. It is intriguing to imagine the brother and sister deciding to submit their work and impressive to think they both survived the selection process. Perhaps Louisa tried again in 1851 and 1852 when her brother is recorded as exhibiting, but if so, she did not get past the jury. Important watercolour exhibiting organisations like the Old Watercolour Society allowed lady amateurs of required standard to show, and some did, distinguished by the name of 'honorary exhibitor'. These were usually upper class women who had been taught by well known painters of the day. Professional female painters like the Mrs. Green who possibly taught Louisa also exhibited, of course, using the publicity to bring in the pupils and commissions which were their bread and butter. In 1851 the first exhibition of the Society of Amateur Artists was held. The 'amateur' in the title encouraged many women to submit their work and all the reviewers noted the large proportion of female exhibitors.

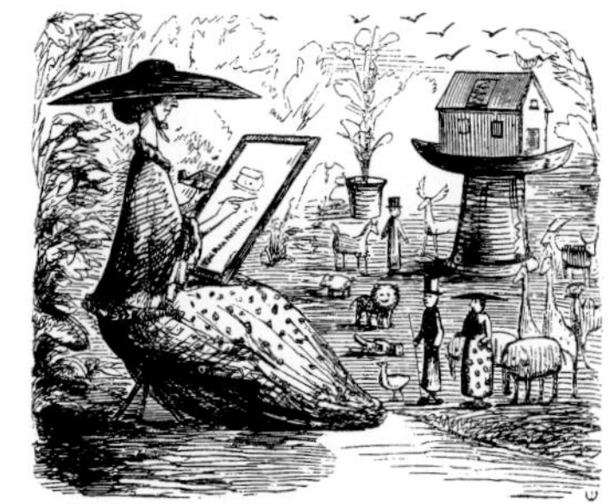

SKETCHING FROM NATURE.

Miss Raphael makes a study for her grand Picture, "The Day after the Deluge."

Fig.3 Punch, 29 September 1849

The reviews tell us a lot about contemporary attitudes to the female amateurs. In mid Victorian England, amateur, when used in conjunction with female, was a derogatory concept. Women, it was believed, were inferior painters because they relied too heavily on copying; because they did not learn perspective properly; and because, though they could respond to a landscape, they could not idealise it – in other words, they lacked imagination. Even the reviewers' compliments have their sting. The works of ladies are "predominantly superior to those of the men as will and must be the case where the untutored dictates of taste and expression are consulted" wrote the critic of the Literary Gazette in 1852. "In justness of feeling, closeness of observation and of facility of rendering in the early stages of the art, no one questions the pre-eminence of female capabilities." Decoded, this means women are good at a sensitive and superficial response to the object; just don't ask them to produce anything dazzling in the way of more sustained work. The cartoon from *Punch* says it all *(Fig 3)*. The fact that by mid century, when Louisa did her paintings, the young Queen and a number of aristocratic women were watercolourists carried no weight in this debate where amateur (bad) was pitched against professional (good).

It is hardly fair to blame the women for their low standing. The reasons for learning to draw in the educational manuals all have one fascinating feature in common: they never mention the development of

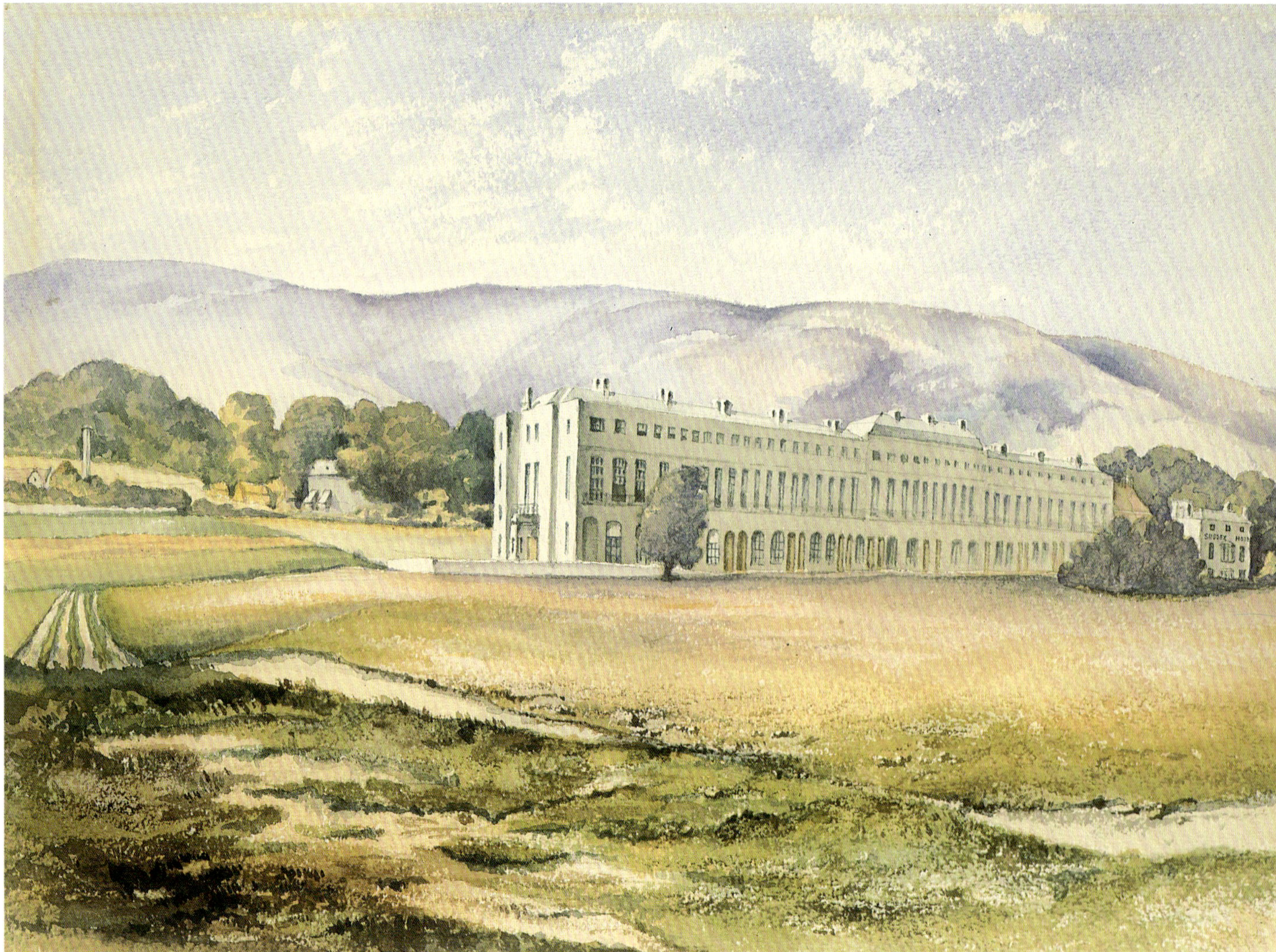

24 *Cornfield Terrace, Eastbourne. 1852*

artistic skills. Drawing is always done for other reasons. It teaches observation, which "is of infinitely more value…than all the actual productions of female artists since the world began", writes Mrs. Ellis. It is quiet: "however defective the performance may be, it does not necessarily, like music, jar upon the sense." It helps maintain "that general cheerfulness which is a part of social and domestic duty". Most important of all it helps a girl get a husband. Since it did not work this magic for Louisa, it is comforting to read her father's defence of spinsters in *Philosophy in Sport Made Science in Earnest.* On the evidence of this parental attitude, it is possible that the four of the five Paris sisters who remained unmarried escaped any feelings of shame about their spinster state.

The mixed messages sent to the female student did not encourage excellence. On the one hand she was told that accomplishments were necessary and admired, and on the other she was warned against becoming too good since "any girl of eighteen who without rare genius has attained a high degree of excellence in any art, must have done so at the expense of studies which ought to have occupied the time given to the accomplishment". Putting yourself forward was a Victorian female sin. Announced the author of *The Daughters of England*: "As women, then, the first thing of importance is to be content to be inferior to men – inferior in mental power, in the same proportion that you are inferior in bodily strength." Women artists, whether amateur or professional, practised art at mid century against a background of these beliefs. The miracle is that so many managed to produce good work.

The drawings of the villages to the north west of London in the 1833 sketchbook show a recognisable Louisa Paris (**2**). Already her taste was for painting what was in front of her eyes rather than painting from her imagination. The delicacy of the watercolours is already present in the sensitively varied range of marks in the drawings done twenty years earlier. The simple frontal compositions show her resistance to the glamourising compositional formulae of the manuals, a refusal to doctor reality which is still with her years later. While not claiming any originality for her compositions, which tend to either recede in horizontal bands or be cut with a diagonal, her interest in accurate reproduction means that compositional

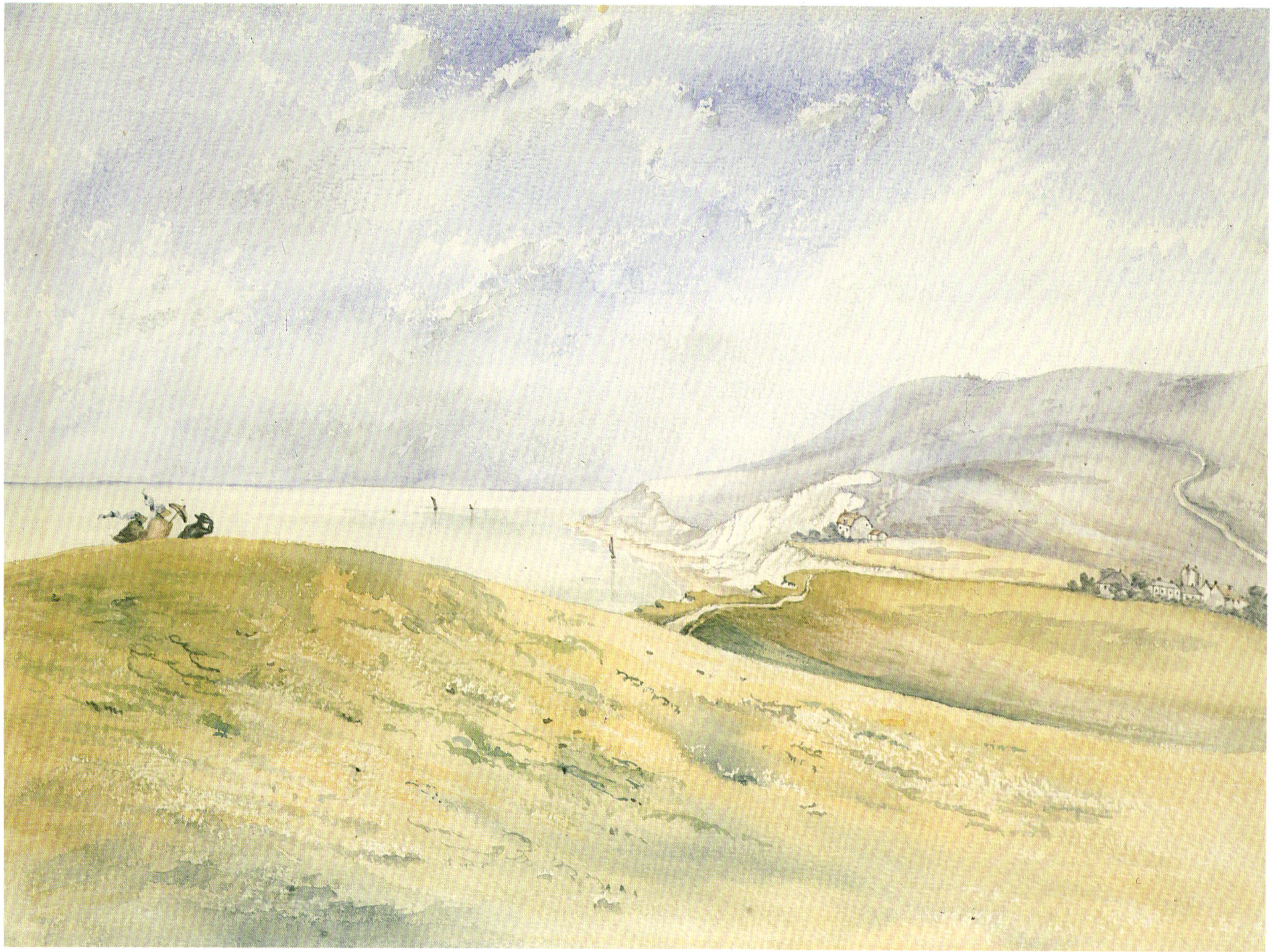

26 *Sketch on the cliff of the villages of Meads and Holywell, and Beachy Head in the distance. obliged to return home on account of rain.*

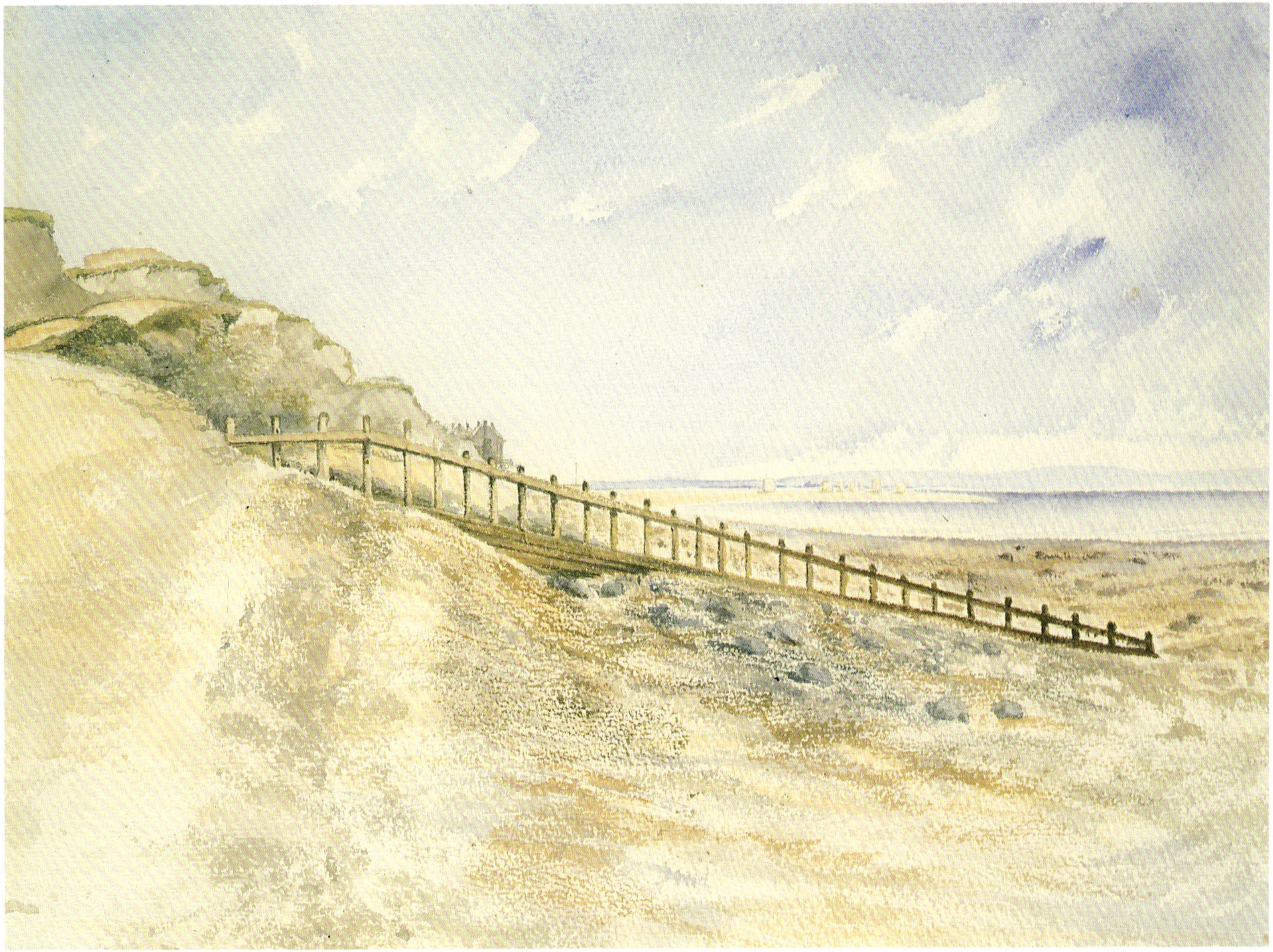

32 *Sketched for the sake of the remembrance, in ten minutes, the first of the Sea houses in the distance, whilst we were at Eastbourne they were nearly washed away! Ellen and I sketched in the afternoon. Sepr. 1852. Louisa C Paris.*

clichés are mostly ignored. Even her few descents into conventional framing devices like views through arched trees or trellis are saved from looking trite by her resolve to paint exactly what she sees. She doubtless continued to develop the portrait skills shown in the second sketchbook (**4**), although the only portrait in the Towner collection is the *"very bad likeness of Mrs. Watson"* (**17**) – oh, that female self deprecation; if it was really so poor, why did she keep it?.

With the first sea paintings, the compositional format changes so dramatically from the frontal pattern of the earlier Cockfield scenes to an altogether more dashing affair of diagonals, that they could be by a different hand. Her power to suggest distance is also released by the sea, the vistas expressed in increasingly faded washes and bands. The tones in the sketch of Saltwood Castle (**64**) so sensitively evoke the distance that the viewer is lured through the gate into the field and then up on to the downs beyond.

Enchanting paintings, or even a patch of enchantment in a very ordinary painting, make one wonder what a demanding teacher would have made of her talent. The quality is bewilderingly uneven. The sketch of Sproughton Rectory (**47**) is compositionally crude yet the Brockman Summer-House (**74**) presents a ravishing set of horizontal strips of brown, yellow, blue, spinach and yellowy green.

An attractive artistic personality comes off these paintings. She tries things out: experiment is the only acceptable explanation for the scrubby dry texture of the paint dragged over the foreground of some of her paintings – effective in suggesting the patchy quality of the ground in Cornfield Terrace (**24**) but unattractive in the view of Eastbourne towards Beachy Head (**25**). She is amused by the everyday and there is obvious enjoyment in her depictions of scarves that fly joyously in the wind or of sheep seen squarely from behind. Back views are something of a Louisa Paris trademark, one which was already visible two decades earlier in the sketchbook (**2**). Since the second sketchbook proves that this quirk does not stem from any lack of ability to draw figures, it must be recognised as a defining feature of Louisa Paris' work.

There is a remarkable sense of the painter's presence in these watercolours. The strongest signals come from the stool, umbrella, palette and paintbox which occur in several of the paintings and make up a sort of self portrait, a way of painting herself into the landscape (**35**, **65**, **68**). Even more revealing are

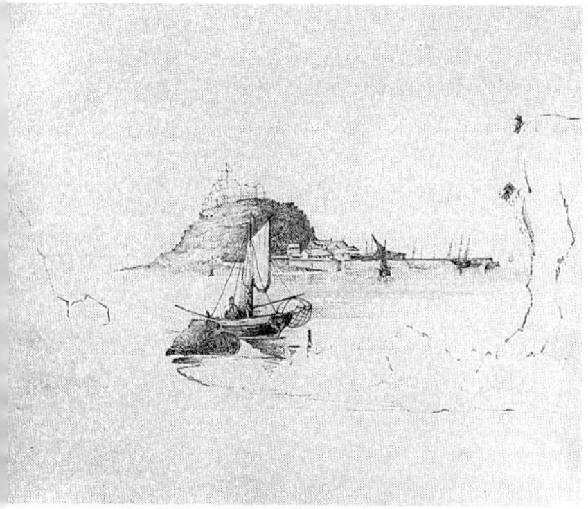

2.1 Fishing boat set against fishing village. Pencil sketch.

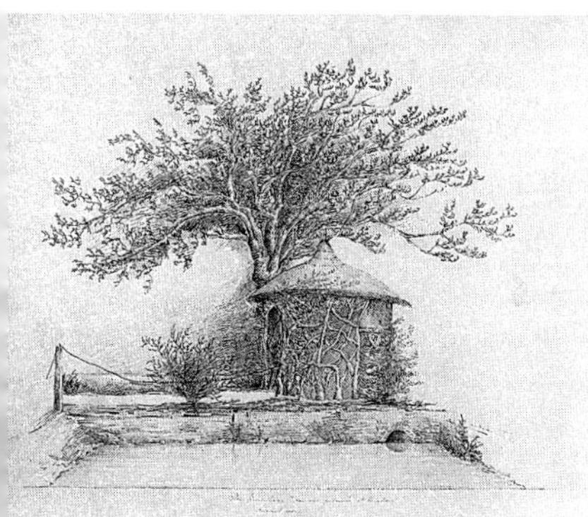

2.2 *The Hermitage in our grounds at Hendon August 1833.* Pencil sketch.

the comments written under the pictures in her neatest handwriting. (The notes scrawled at the time of painting on the backs of the watercolours are much untidier.) They add immeasurably to the impact of the paintings, turning them into a visual diary. The story they tell is of a woman whose life is centered on family and friends and for whom watercolour is less an accomplishment than a brilliant means of social intercourse and a way of adding pleasure and purpose to her days.

Days were organised around expeditions in which all or some of the party sketched. Her father is only mentioned once, but how satisfying that when he is he has spent a day sketching Pevensey Castle with his daughter: no time for generational awkwardness when absorbed in painting scenery. She rarely worked alone, in part because she was with friends and family, but also because the nineteenth century disapproved of the unchaperoned middle class woman. One of the rare times she can paint unaccompanied is from her bedroom window: we have the view from her bedroom (**7**) matched by the one of the back of the Rectory which looks up towards the bedroom (**9**).

A faint scent of past pleasures wafts up from the comments. A day among the ruins at Pevensey Castle is *"delightful"*. Returning home from Beachy Head she sees mushrooms underfoot and a sunset overhead. There are excitements: on a sketching excursion, Mrs. Walker finds a brooch she lost five or seven years before. And there are adventures: sketching at Eastbourne, they are frightened by a madman.

The captions suggest that Louisa was her mother's closest companion, perhaps because she was the oldest daughter. She stays with her while the others go off sketching: *"The beach Eastbourne, taken late in the evening, Mama and myself having been alone all day, the rest of the party having gone to Beachy Head."* She notes her mother's outing to Beachy Head as *"a tremendous walk for her"*. A drawing is done while staying with her mother at a hotel on Weybridge Common, Surrey: *"Mama's cough was so bad I went with her for a week, enjoyed it very much."* The sense of family closeness is so strong that she must have been devastated by her mother's death in 1855 and her father's in 1856.

The captions are revealing in other ways, too. On the back of her painting of Cockfield Church (**11**) she wrote: *"Miss Latter kindly brought her maid to carry all my sketching things back – it being extremely hot –"*

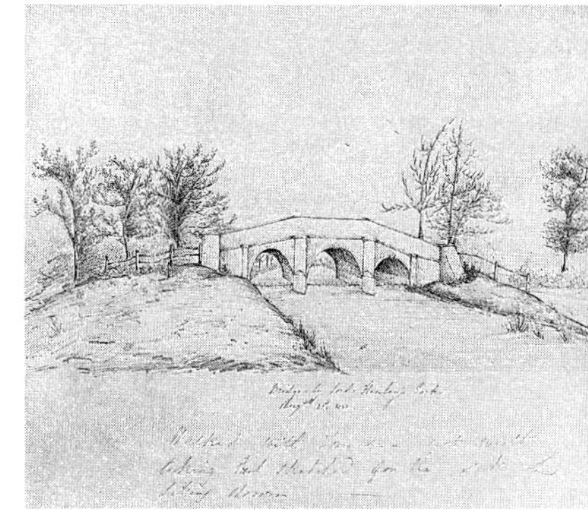

2.3 *Bridge by Lord Henley's Park. Augst 21st 1833. Walked with Tom – not worth taking but sketched for the sake of sitting down.* Pencil sketch.

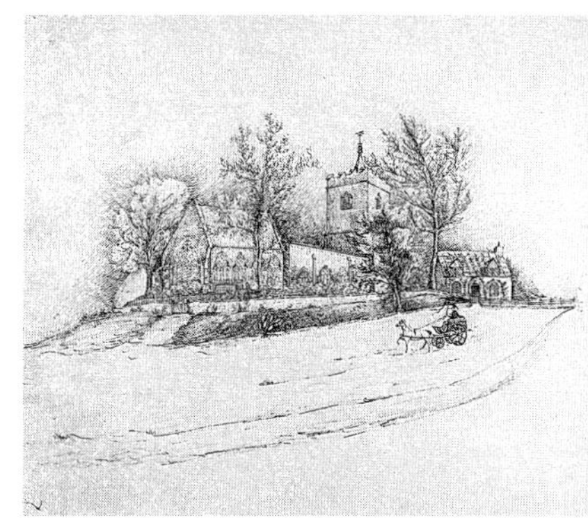

2.4 Cottage and church with horse and cart in foreground. Pencil sketch.

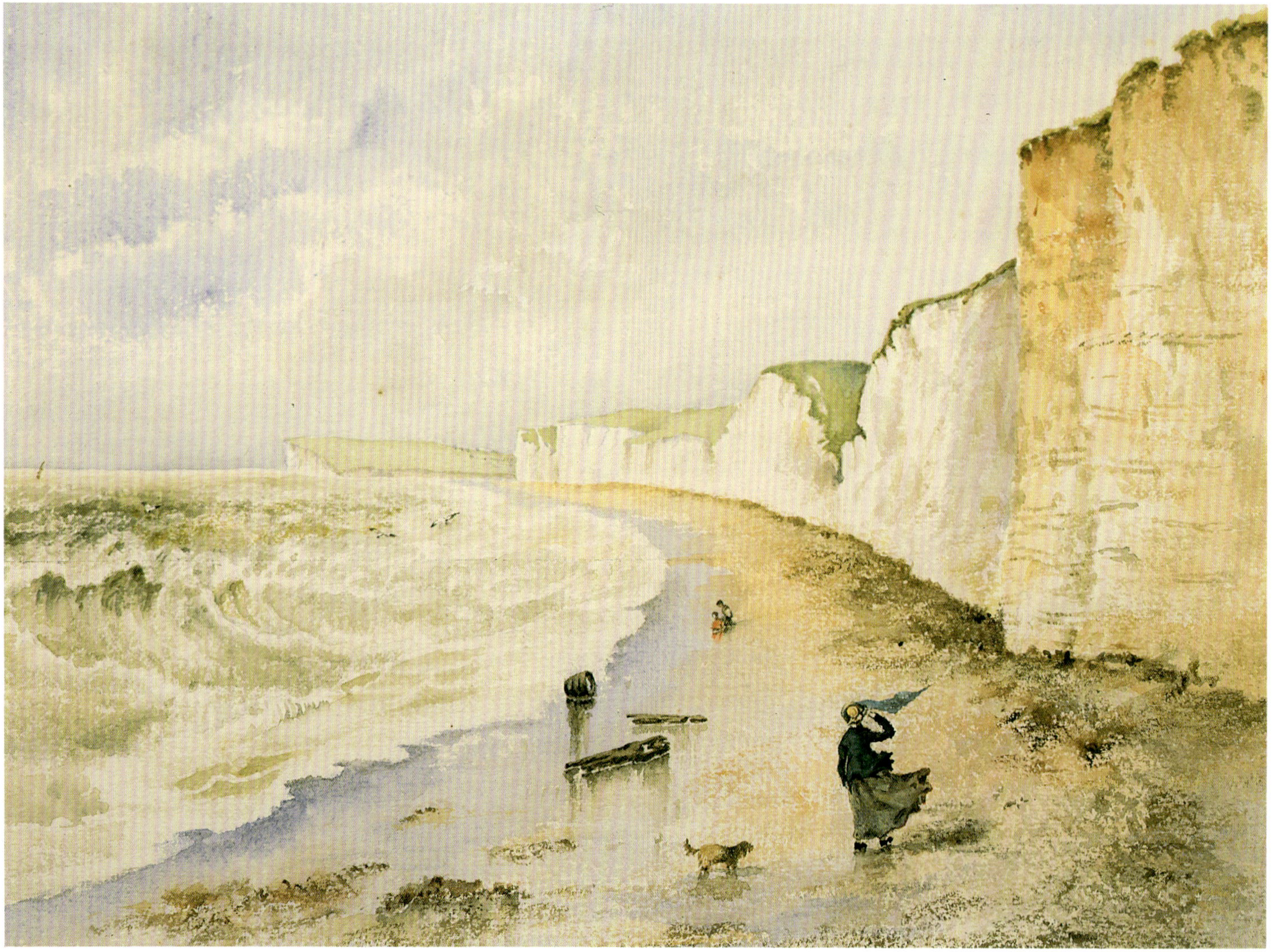

44 *Burling* (sic) *Gap, Sep*^{r}*. 30*th*. 1852. magnificent cliffs further on towards Beachy Head, quite "perpendicular"! Ellen and Muff trying to stand against the gale!*

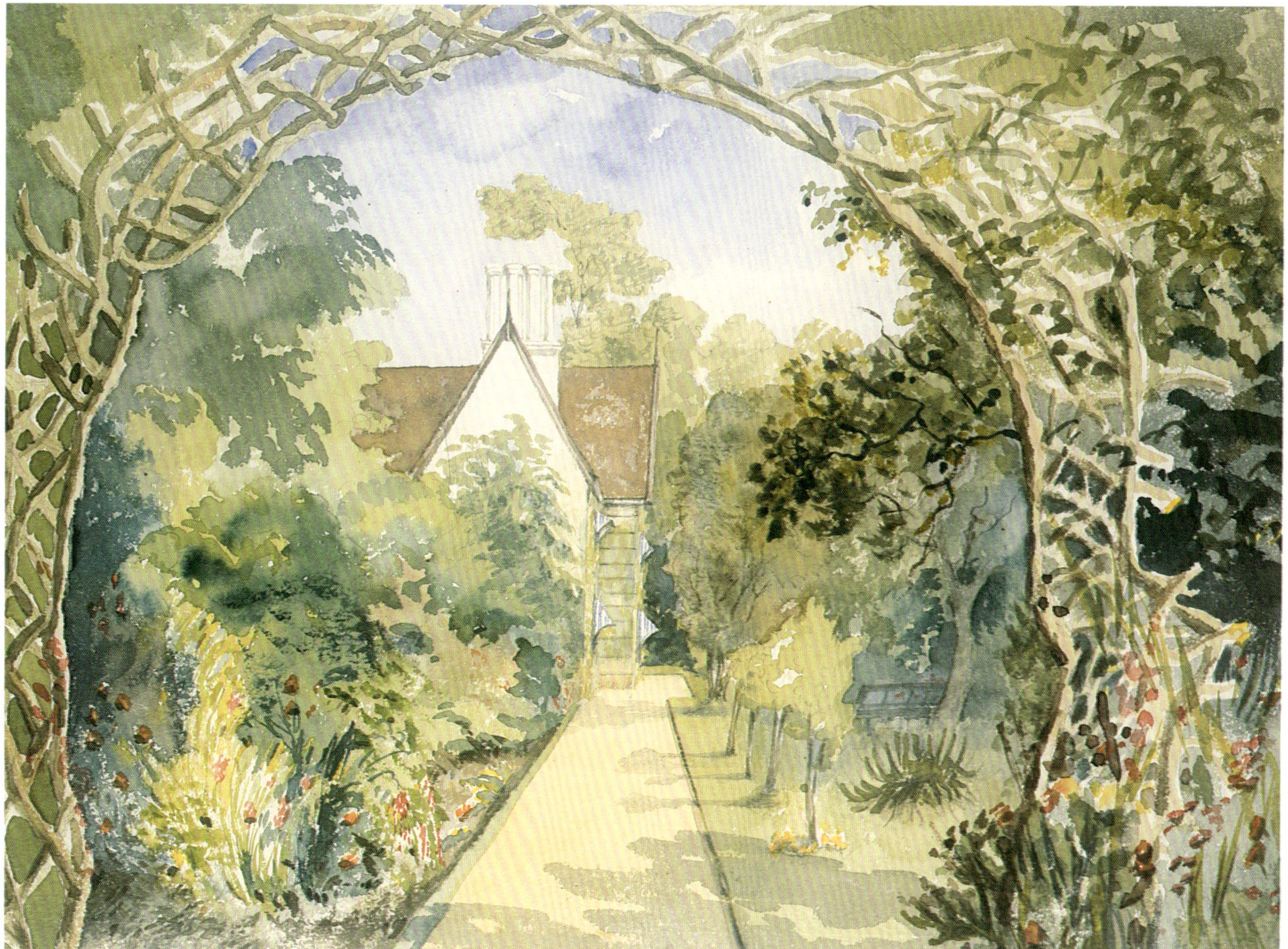

47 *Sproughton Rectory, from the end of the walk. 1853.*

This did not get transferred to the front of the picture: just as there were servants' quarters in the homes there were servants' places in art – on the back of the painting, not the front.

One of the fascinations of this body of work by Louisa Paris is the way it escapes the patronising attitudes which both our century and hers heap on the lady amateurs. A poorly trained amateur? Perhaps, but think of the pleasure her paintings gave herself, her family, her friends and us, a century and a half later. A mere accomplishment? True, but also a daily practice, at least in summer, and a means of adding richness to a quiet existence. Louisa Paris lies midway between the dilettante girls who learned to draw to help them catch a husband and the women who ambitiously showed at the watercolour exhibitions. She painted to enhance her leisure, give a point to her life and bring pleasure to her friends and family circle. It is our good fortune, and one she would never have imagined, that her paintings also offer us an insight into the role played by art in a mid-Victorian lady's life.

Frances Borzello

Further Reading

A Struggle for Fame – Victorian Women Artists and Authors, Yale Centre for British Art, New Haven 1994

Deborah Cherry, *Painting Women*, London 1993

Michael Clarke, *The Tempting Prospect*, London 1981

Mrs Ellis, *The Daughters of England*, London 1842

J Friedman, *Every Lady Her Own Drawing Master,* Apollo, vol. 105, no. 182, 1977, pp 262-267

Catherine F Newman, *Practical Hints on Female Education,* London 1824

Pamela Gerrish Nunn, *Victorian Women Artists,* London 1987

Emily Shirreff, *Intellectual Education and Its Influence on the Character and Happiness of Women,* London 1858

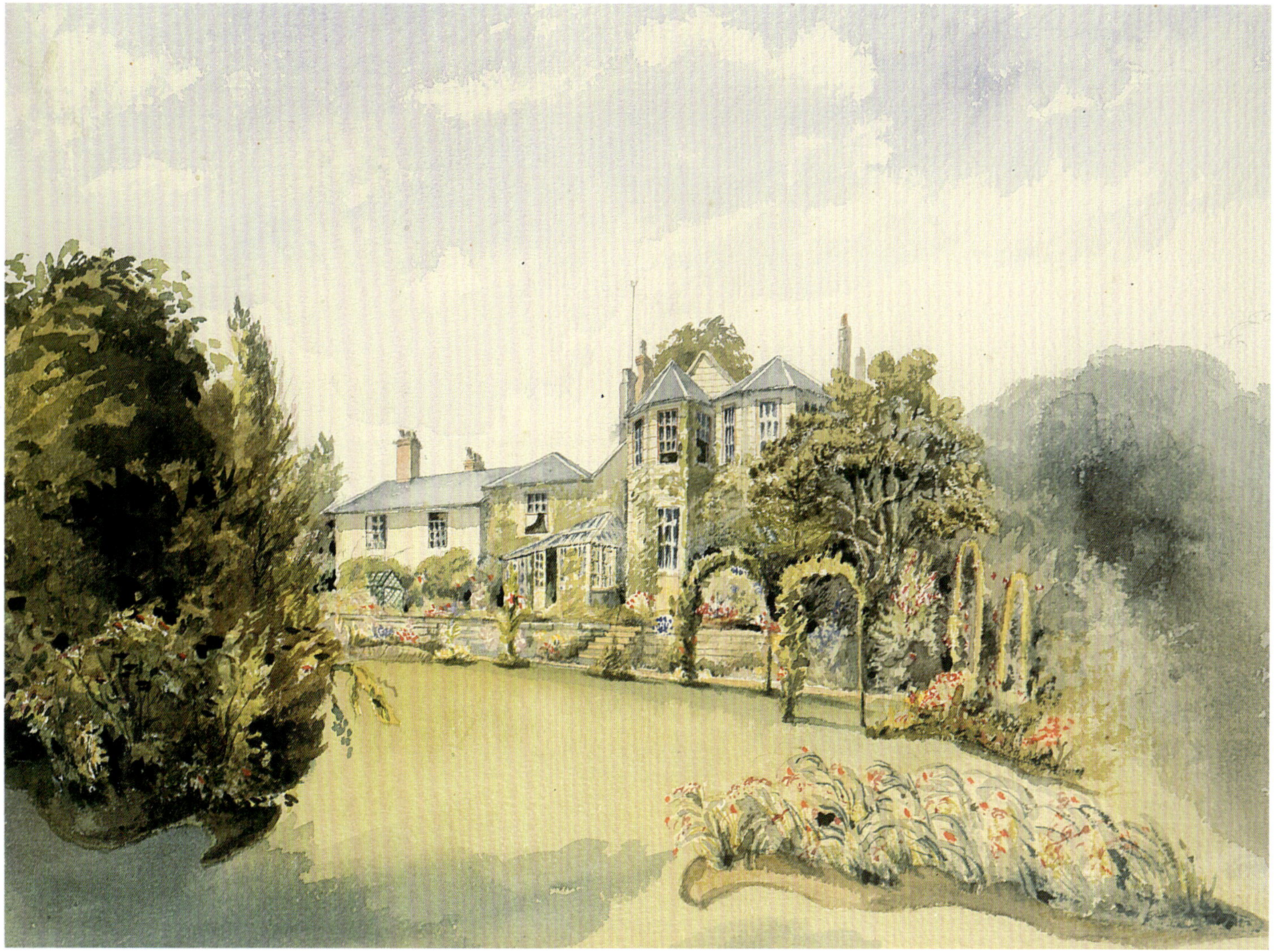

49 *Miss Cresswell's House, Penshurst, Kent, 1853. spent a very pleasant fortnight with her before going to Suffolk, Tom returned from the Mediterranean.*

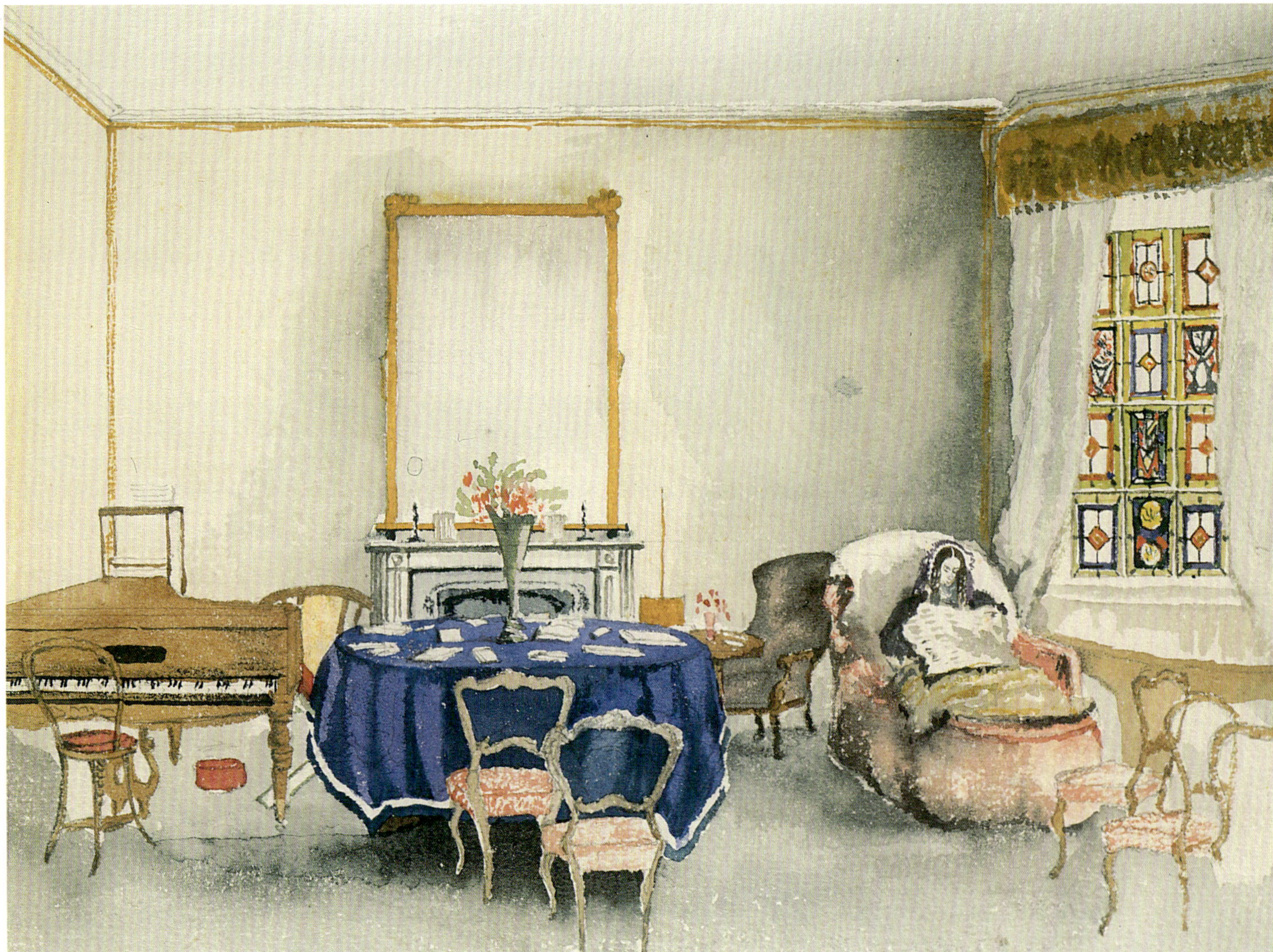

51 *Part of the Penshurst drawing-room, taken in ten minutes, before I left Miss Cresswell in 1853.*

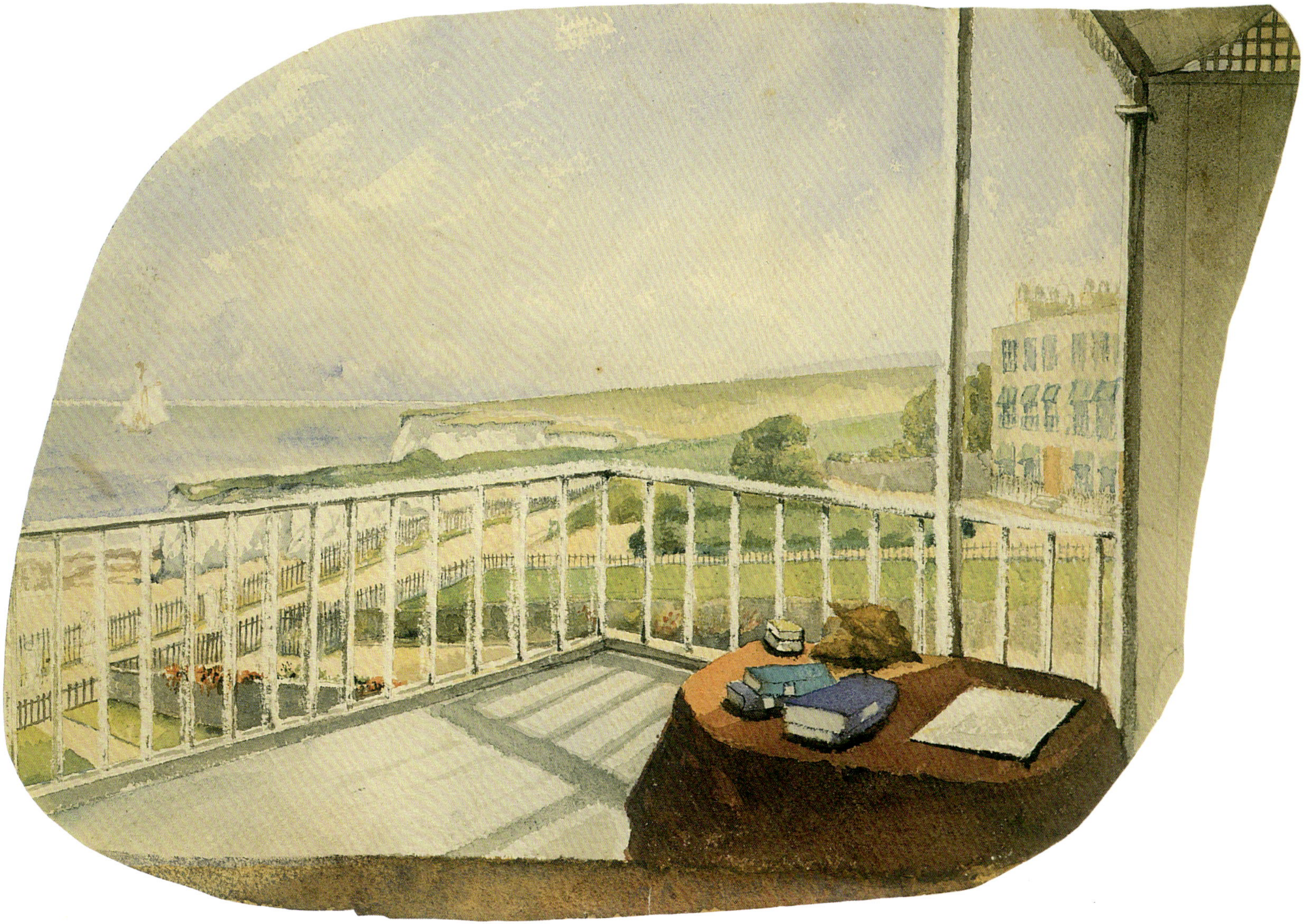

56 Inscribed on reverse: *From the Balcony of Barnes' Library Broadstairs.*

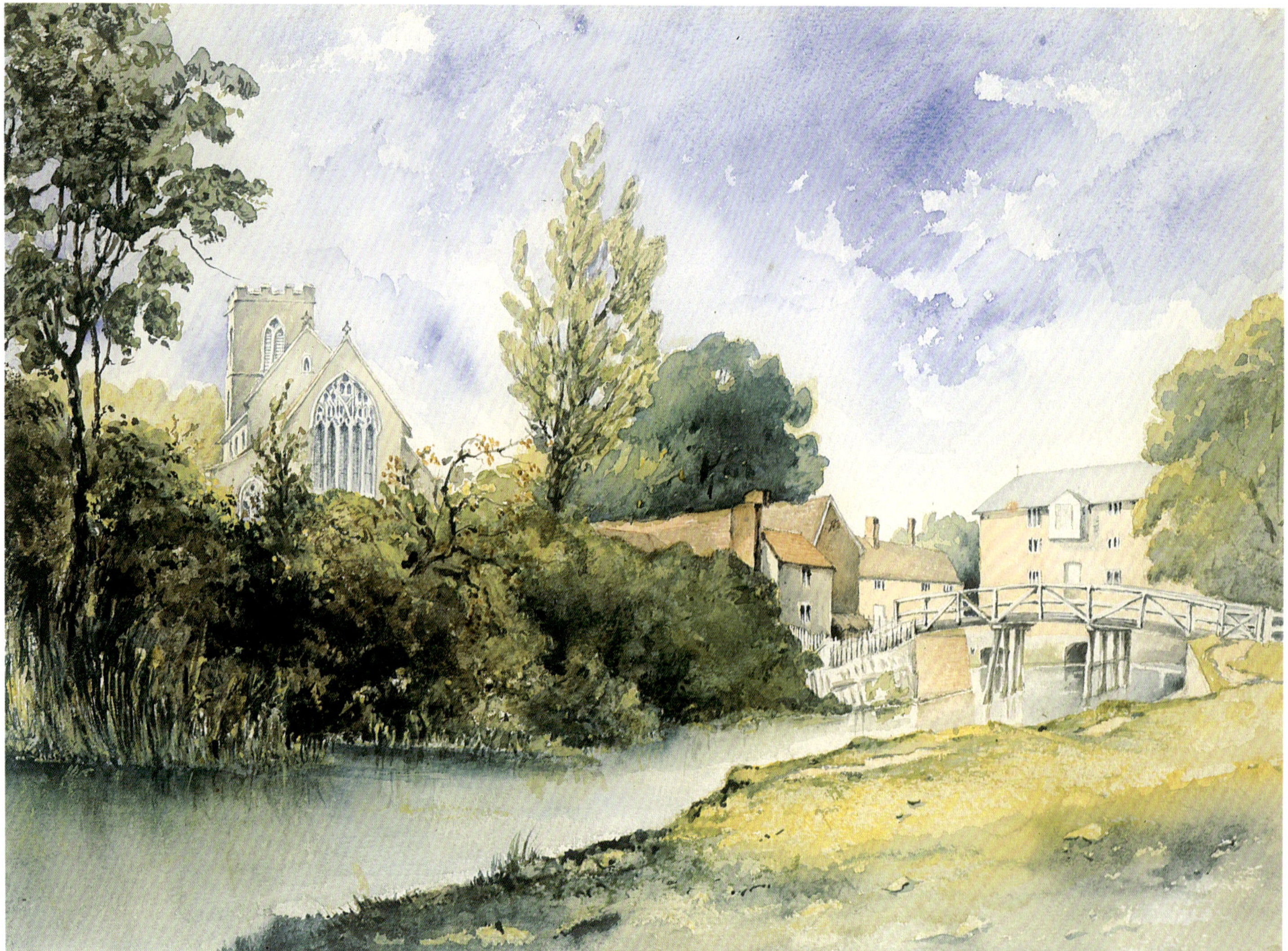

63 *Sproughton Church, and Mill, 10th. August 1854. I went to stay at Sproughton on the 7th, from Cockfield. & left for London on the 12th.*

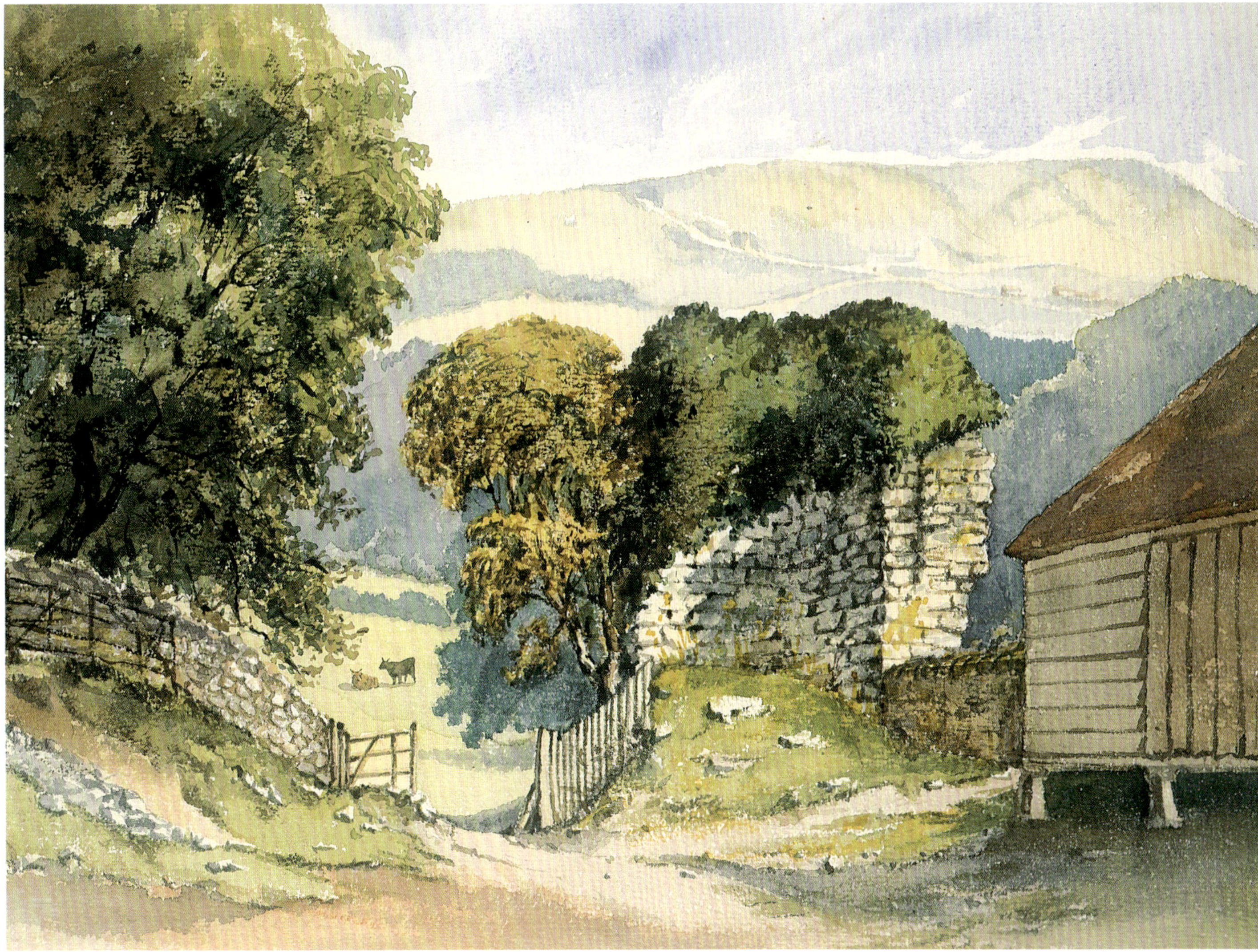

64 *Sketch from Saltwood Castle, 22nd. of Septr. walked into the wood afterwards.*

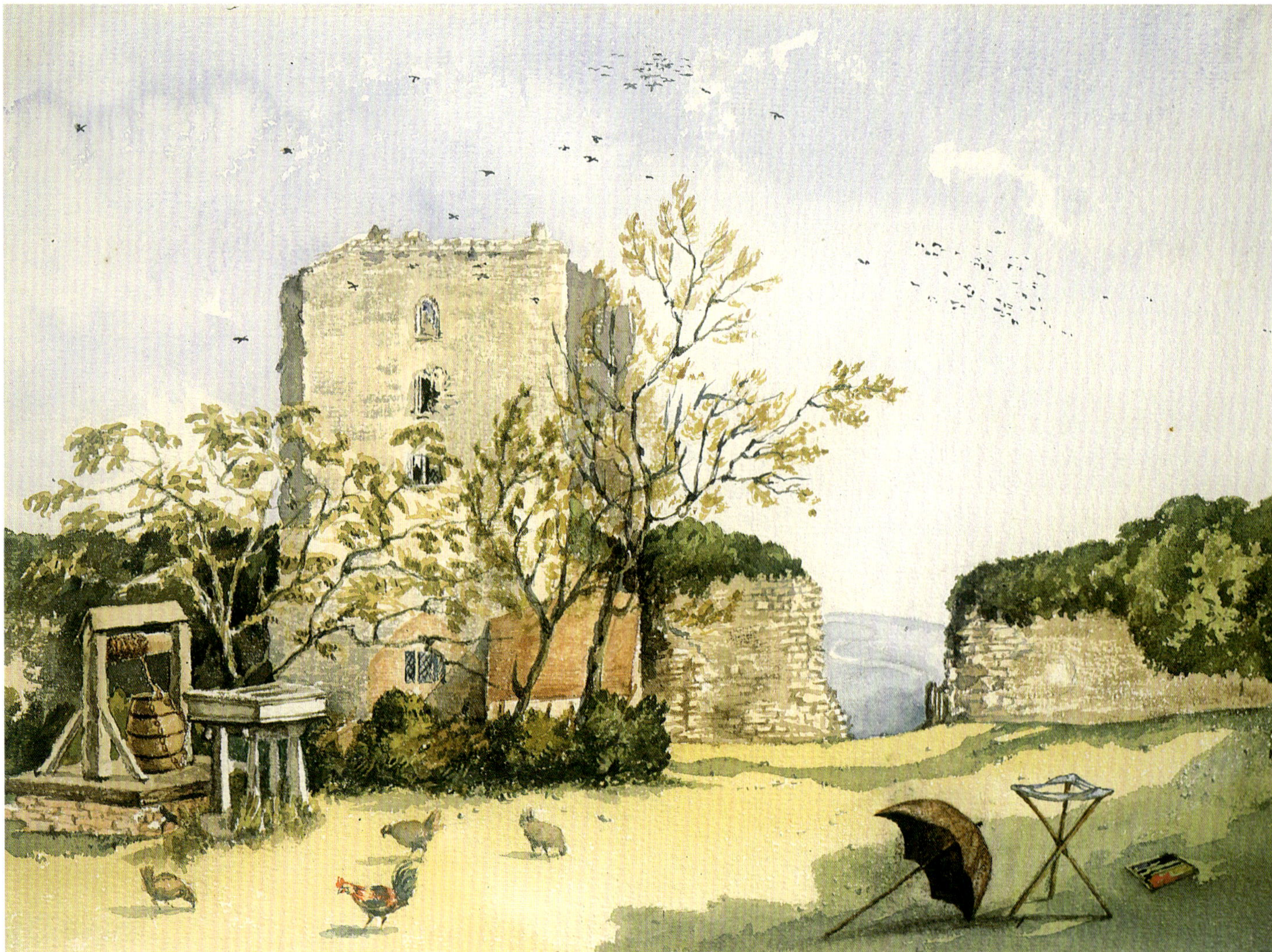

65 *Saltwood, Mama and Fanny came late with Muffy. Tom and Ellen sketched from the top of the wall. Ellen took a likeness of Tom.*

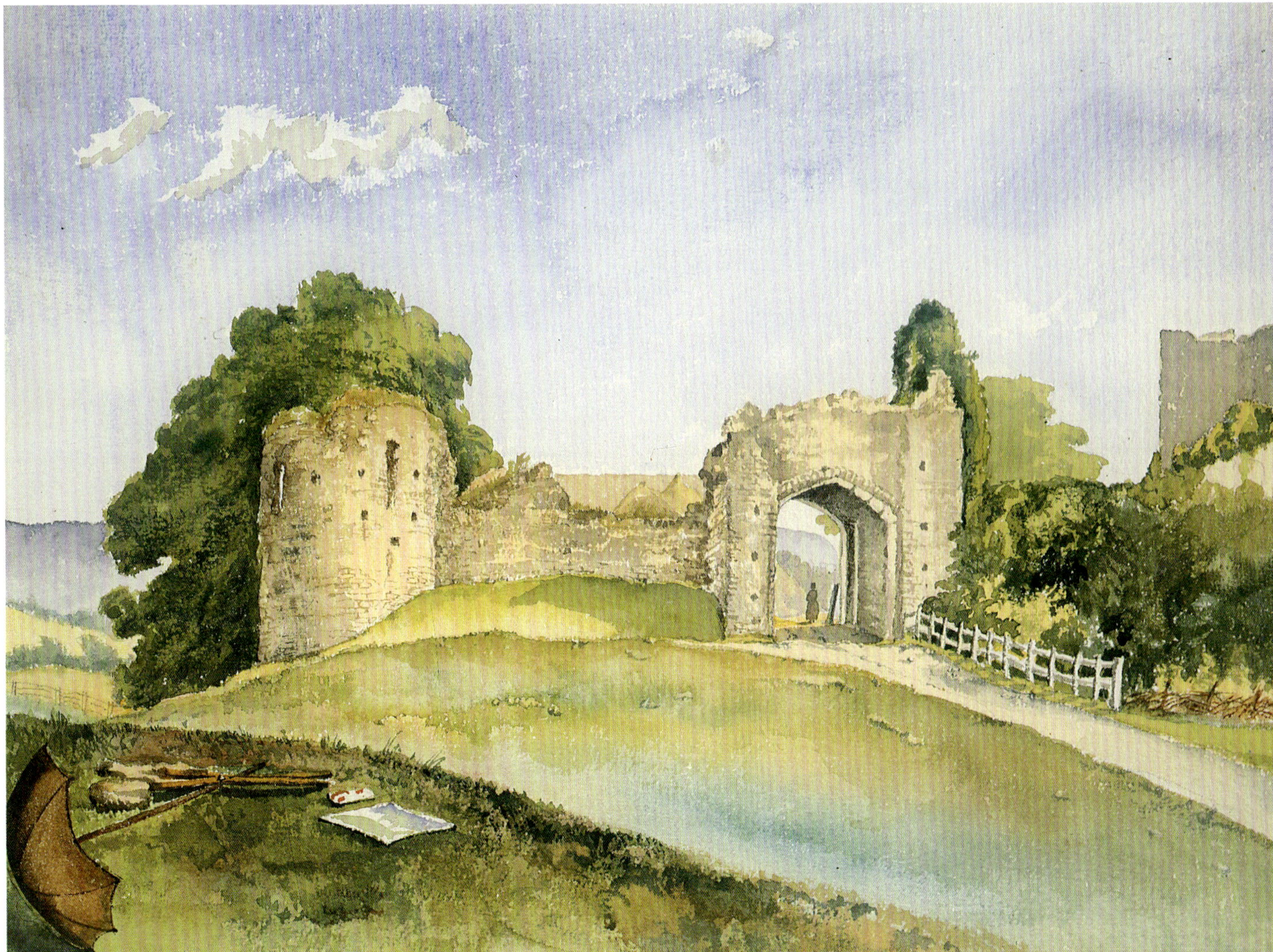

67 *Rosa, Ellen & I walked early to Saltwood & sketched the entrance gate. Mama & Fanny met Miss Kingston & joined us afterwards. beautiful day.*

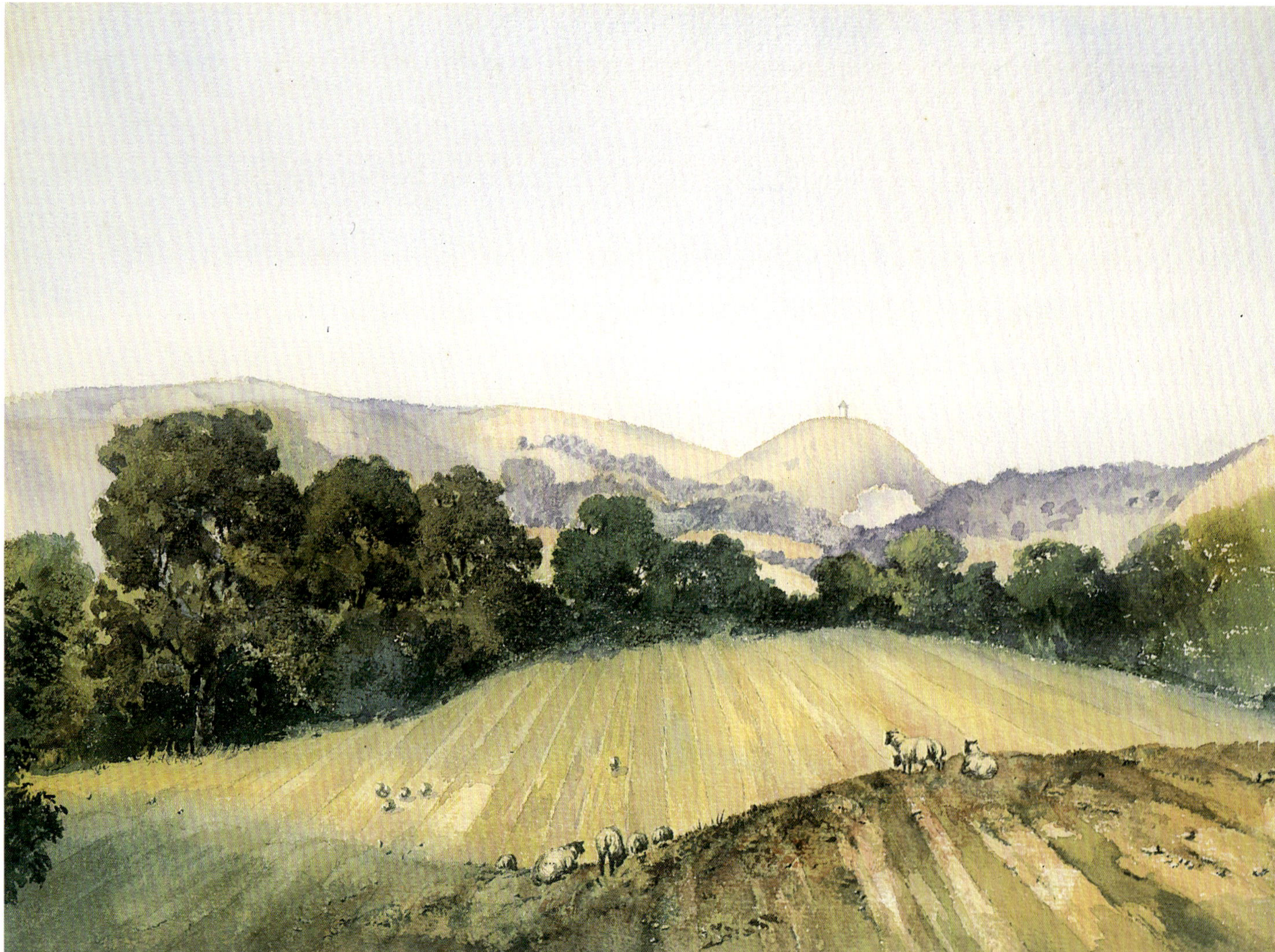

74 *Brockman summer-house at the top of Beechborough Down, near Saltwood. sketched after the dew began to fall.*

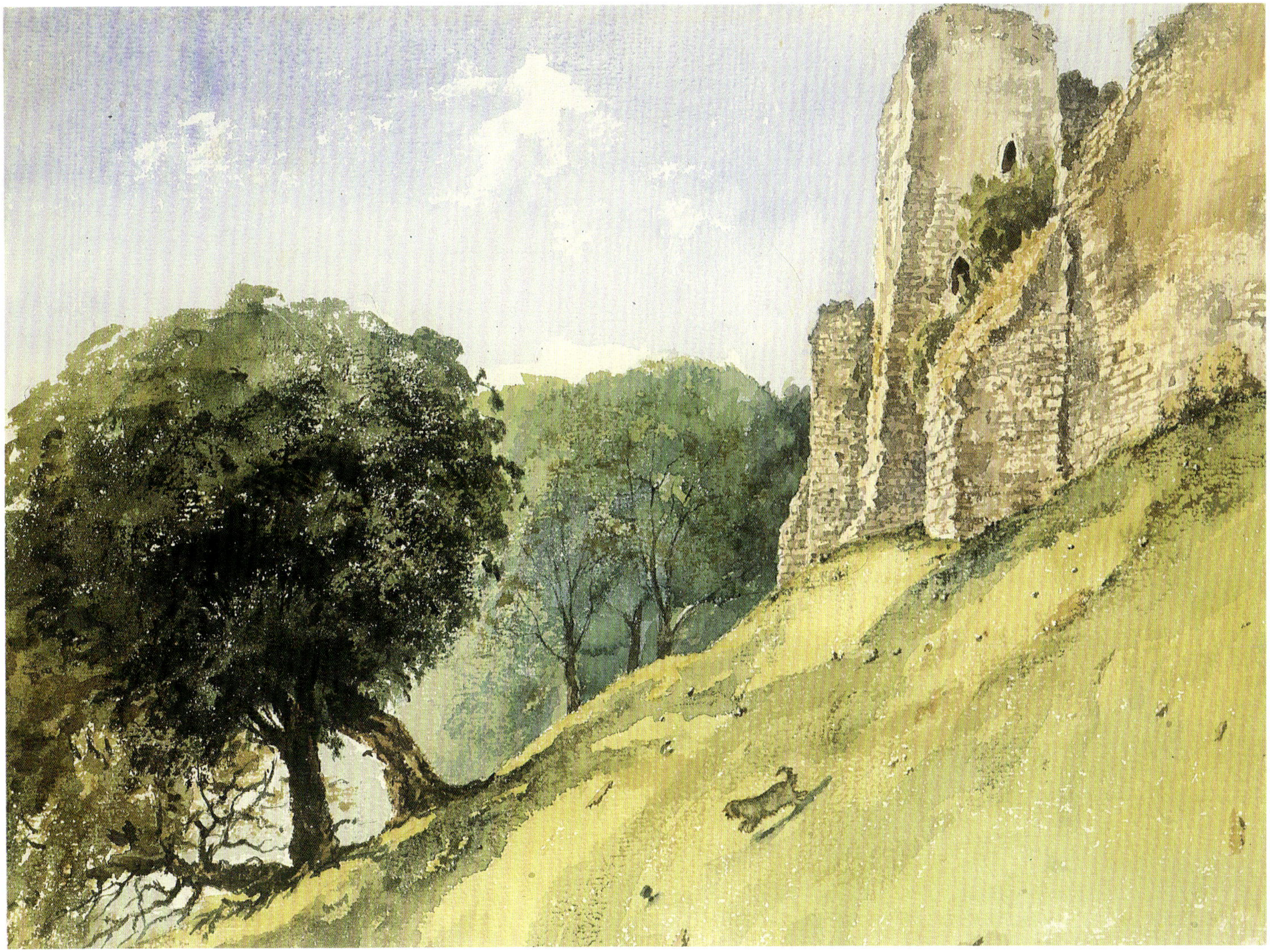

75 *A part of Saltwood Castle, spent the day there as usual, more like June than Oct. from the great heat.*

Catalogue

Measurements are in centimetres, height precedes width. Numbers in brackets refer to the page number on which the work is illustrated.

1 *Portrait of Dr. John Ayrton Paris* 1832 (11)
Oil on ivory
11.9 x 15
Inscribed on verso: *Louisa Cath. Paris Pinxit Dover Street, Feb^{ry} 25th 1832.*
Private Collection

2 Unbound and incomplete sketchbook of 23 pencil drawings, 1833 (28,29)
Paper watermarked 1830
23.2 x 29.3
Private Collection

3 *Self Portrait (?)* 1835 (frontispiece)
Oil on ivory
Inscribed on reverse: *L.C. Paris. Painted for and given to Papa 1835 by his affect(ionate) Louisa.*
8.5 x 6.7
Private Collection

4 Green leather bound sketchbook with watercolour and pencil drawings, 1837-49
23.6 x 19.2
Private Collection

The following are watercolour on paper, measuring 24.5 x 34.5 unless otherwise stated. The titles in italics are inscriptions written by Louisa Paris below the watercolours, unless otherwise stated. When the inscription on the reverse differs from the caption on the front, it is also given. The watercolours were bought in 1960 by the Towner Art Gallery from a family who inherited them from Louisa Paris' brother, Thomas Paris.

1852

Suffolk

5 *Cockfield Rectory, sat with Miss Latter by the Moat to sketch it a day or two after I arrived. June. 52. LC Paris.*

6 *M^{r}. and M^{rs}. Watson, Mary and Grace, and their dog Frank. Cockfield 1852.*

7 *View from my bedroom, Cockfield, got up very early and sketched before breakfast. 1852. Louisa C Paris* – (6)

8 *Front of the Rectory, Cockfield, Suffolk. June 1852. sketched half way between the gate and house. Louisa Cath^{ne}. Paris.*

9 *Back of Rectory, Cockfield, sat out under the trees sketching with Mrs. Watson – 'till luncheon, driven in by a violent thunder-storm. very warm day! June 1852.* (7)

10 *The Lime trees, and one of the entrance gates. Cockfield Rectory, Suffolk. Louisa Catherine Paris. July 1852.*

11 *Cockfield Church from one of the fields in the walk to church from the Rectory, July 1852. Louisa C Paris.* (17)
Inscribed on reverse: *Taken from one of the fields in the walk to church from the Rectory – Miss Latter kindly brought her maid to convey all my sketching things back – it being extremely hot –*

12 *Water across the road. Cockfield July 1852., found Mrs. Forbes arrived from the Isle of Man, upon my return from sketching. Louisa C Paris.*
Inscribed on reverse: *Water over the road – Cockfield – walked unknown to the Rectory. People who were hunting everywhere for me – Mrs. Forbes arrived from the Isle of Man.*

13 *The famous fishing place, Cockfield;-intensely hot day!, walked with Mrs. Watson and Miss Latter, Mrs. Latter joined us afterwards. July 1852., Louisa Paris.*

14 *Brenteliegh Church, delightful drive in the cool of the evening, sketched in a hurry, and walked through the park afterwards. July 1852. Louisa C Paris.*
Inscribed on reverse: *...to our horror discovered we must climb a most difficult gate of 12 bars!!!! – Mr. George Watson delighted at our discomfort – –*

15 *Mimus Cross, on the road to Bury. Mrs. Watson, Miss Latter and little Mary Watson. Louisa C Paris. 52.*
Inscribed on reverse: *Mrs. Latter & Mr. Watson were going to Bury – I started down to sketch – but alas no sketches to be had so obliged to take Fisher's house at Mimus Cross! Waited until nearly ten for them – thundering in the distance little Mary with us – and such a good little thing –*

16 *Halsted Green, near Bury. Delightful drive from Cockfield, Mrs. Watson found a brooch she lost there five years before!!! drove round to the church, and then home to tea. Louisa Paris 1852.*
Inscribed on reverse: *Hawstead. Drove in the Britzca with Mrs. and Miss Latter, Mrs. Watson and little Mary – Mr. Watson drove us – Mrs. W. found a brooch she had lost there seven* (sic) *years ago!! After sketching drove on to see the church – & home to tea – they were frightened at discovering little Mary was surrounded by children with whooping cough.*

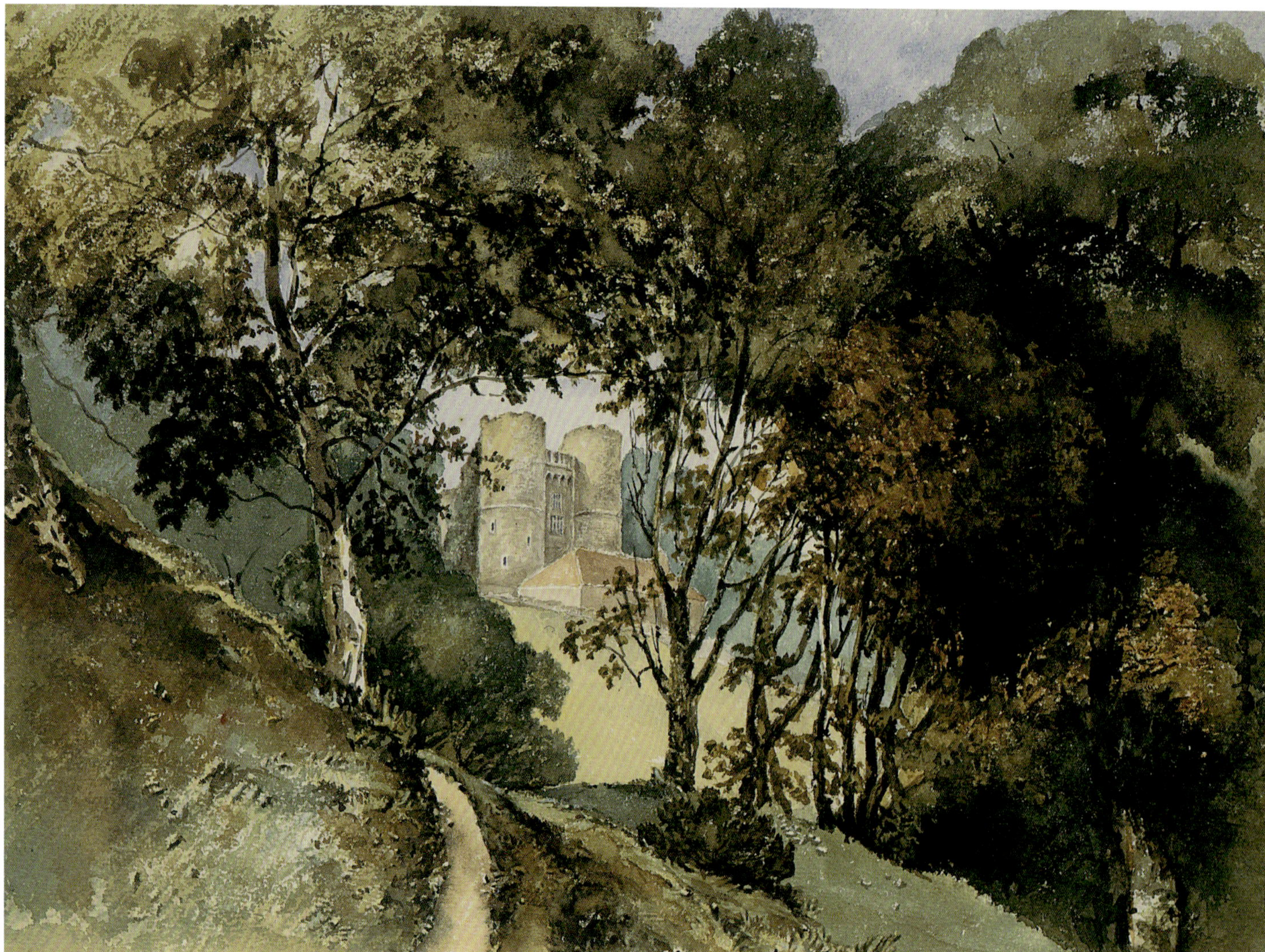

77 *Saltwood, 4th. Octr. the day after Mama left Hythe. finished my sketch in the rain. 1854.*

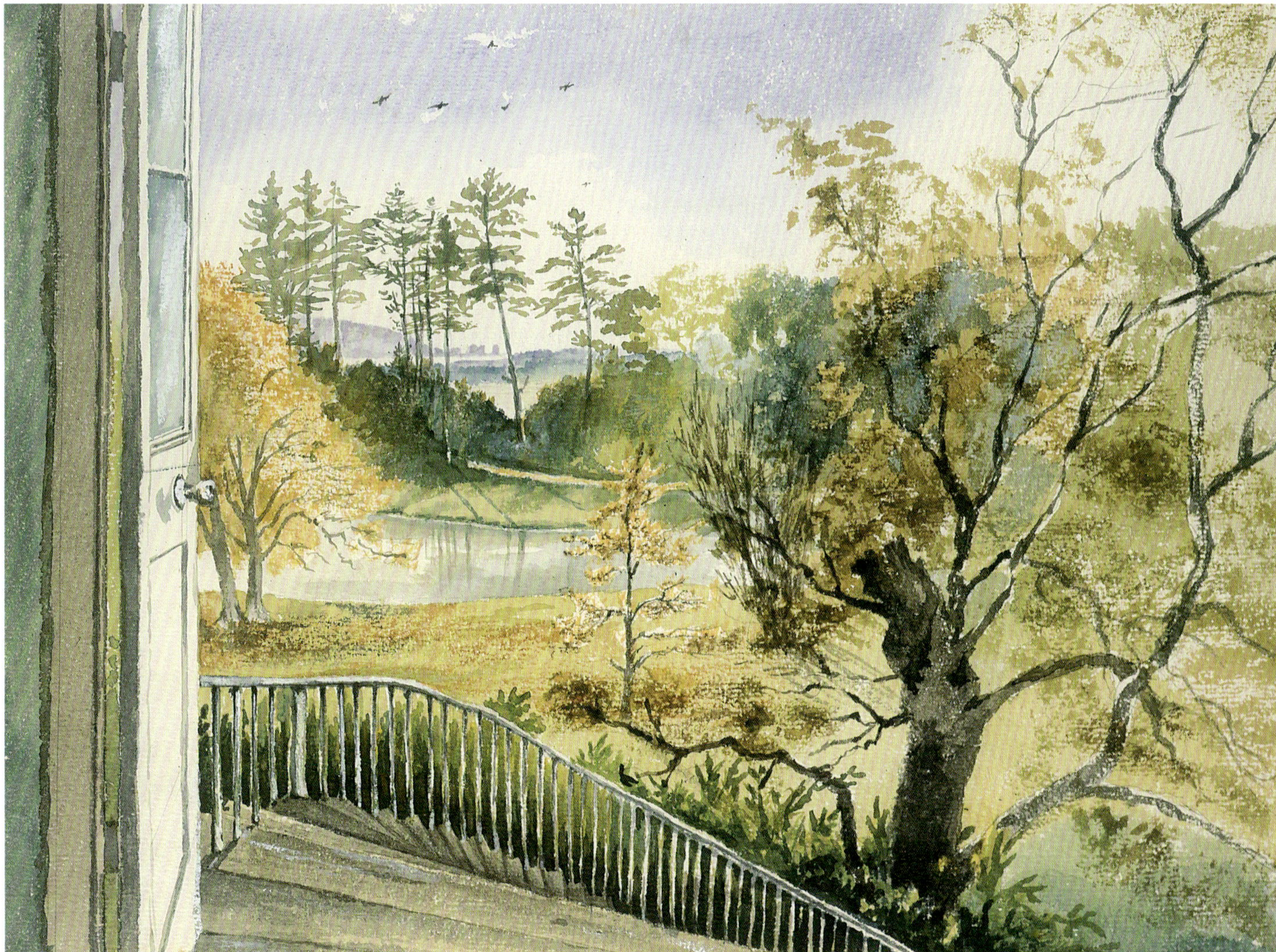

80 *View of the Needles, from the Mount, Walhampton. Novr. 1854. Louisa Paris.*

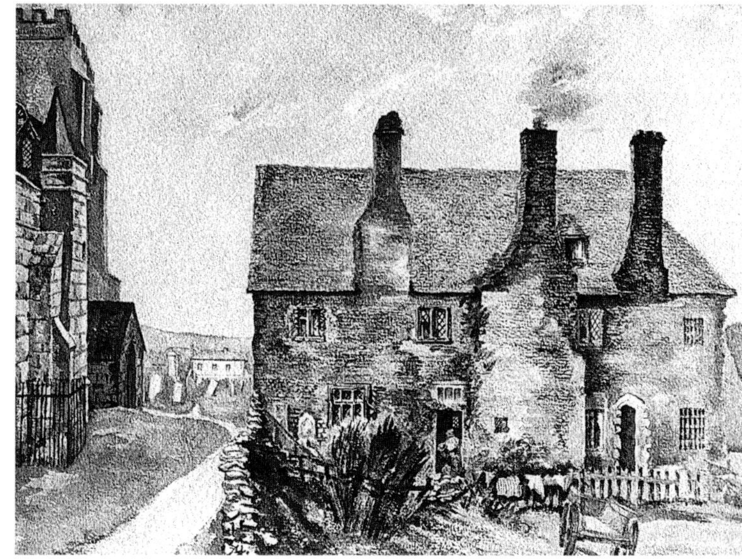

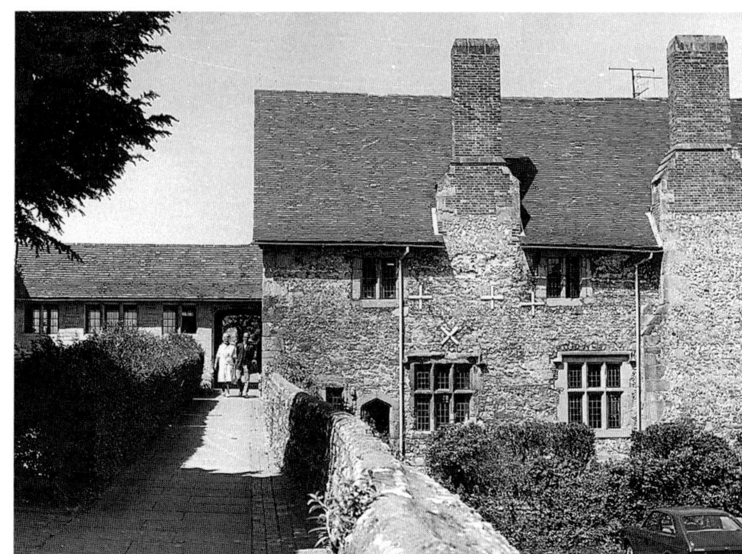

39 *Old cottage and part of Church, old town of Eastbourne, frightened by a madman before we finished our sketch. 17th Sepr. 1852.*
Compared with recent photograph

17 *A very bad likeness of Mrs. Watson.*

18 *Sroughton* (sic) *Church and village, from the bridge. Louisa C Paris July 1852.*

19 *Sproughton, 1852. John Hasted missed the train to take him to Addiscombe and surprised us by returning to tea.*

20 *The School Sproughton, just finished 1852. L.C.P.*

Essex

21 *The Hyde, Mr. Disney's, Essex. I spent a very agreeable three days after my visit into Suffolk in 1852. returned to London on the 7th. Aug. afterwards went to Eastbourne to join Mama & the rest of the party.* (20)

22 *Mr. Disney's suspension bridge. 1852. very slight sketch on account of rain. Louisa C Paris.*

Sussex

23 *Southbourne, sketched from our staircase window at the back of the house. Eastbourne. August 1852.* (21)

24 *Cornfield Terrace. Eastbourne. 1852.* (24)

25 *Eastbourne, from the cliff going up towards Beachy Head. August 1852. Hastings stands at the distant point of land.*

26 *Sketch on the cliff of the villages of Meads and Holywell, and Beachy Head in the distance. obliged to return home on account of rain.* (26)

27 *Beachy Head, from the sands, walked there by the Undercliff.*

28 *The beach Eastbourne, taken late in the evening, Mama and myself having been alone all day, the rest of the party having gone to Beachy Head.*

29 *A sketch of part of Pevensey Castle; drove there with Papa, lovely day, and thoroughly enjoyed the drive, when our sketching was over we discovered, upon wishing to return to Eastbourne, that our conveyance had disappeared! that there was not another to be had in the neighbourhood, not even a cart!! and the last train departed, before we discovered our melancholy situation! at last, at 1/2 past 8 a fly appeared!! our dinner having been ordered at six!! Augst. 23rd 1852*

30 *Cottage of the people who shew* (sic) *the Ruins of Pevensey. Augst. 30th. 1852. Louisa C Paris.*

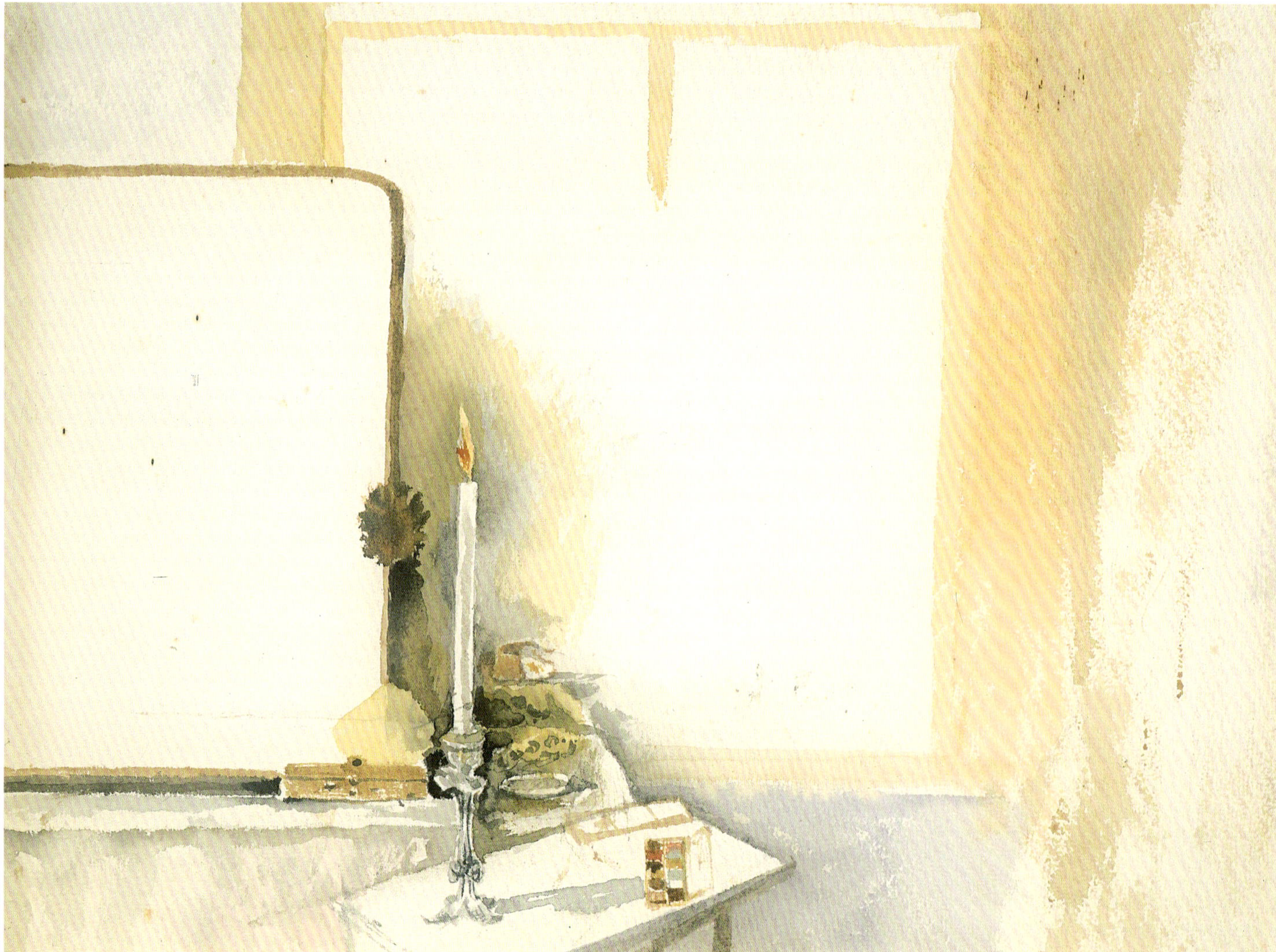

82 Candle.

31 *Part of the ruins of Pevensey Castle, the sea in the distance. spent the day amongst the ruins, and returned to dinner, delightful day. Augst 30th.*

32 *Sketched for the sake of the remembrance, in ten minutes, the first of the Sea houses in the distance, whilst we were at Eastbourne they were nearly washed away! Ellen and I sketched in the afternoon. Sepr. 1852. Louisa C Paris. (27)*

33 *Beach, Eastbourne, taken from the cornfield going up to the Wish Tower. Sepr. 1852.*

34 *Sketched from the beach under the Wish Tower, Eastbourne, my dog Muff my companion, Sepr. 1852.*

35 *The old town of Eastbourne in the valley, taken from the top of the Downs, F, R, E and myself spent the day on the Downs. 4th. Sepr. 1852. taken from the Links Down.*

36 *14th. Sepr. 1852. F, R, E. and myself walked up the Downs towards Beachy Head, very lovely day! E and I sketched, walked afterwards to the Links Down. returned home by seven oclock, finding mushrooms at every step. lovely sunset! dinner on the table when we arrived.*

37 *Chalk Quarry near Eastbourne, I walked there with Mama and John, all the rest of the party having started to spend the day at Burling* (sic) *Gap. Lovely day. and we enjoyed it very much, took our luncheon with us and returned in time for dinner. Sepr. 16th. J's birthday.*

38 *The old town of Eastbourne from the Brighton Road, Mama walked up the Downs with us!!!! 17th. Sepr. 1852.*

39 *Old cottage and part of Church, old town of Eastbourne, frightened by a madman before we finished our sketch. 17th Sepr. 1852.*

40 *Hurstmonceaux Castle Sussex, eleven miles from Eastbourne, passing through Pevensey and Westham, we spent a delightful day in sketching &c. &c. Sep. 24th. 1852. Tom walked, and Muff with him part of the way, and gave him great trouble, being frightened by some large greyhounds, he ran back three miles without stopping! at last, having with much difficulty, caught him in Pevensey, Tom brought him back in M^{r}. Curteis' dog-cart, to whom the Ruins of Hurstmonceaux now belong, – we lunched under the tree.*

41 *South and grand front of Hurstmonceaux Castle, Sussex. 24th Sepr. 1852. Friday.*

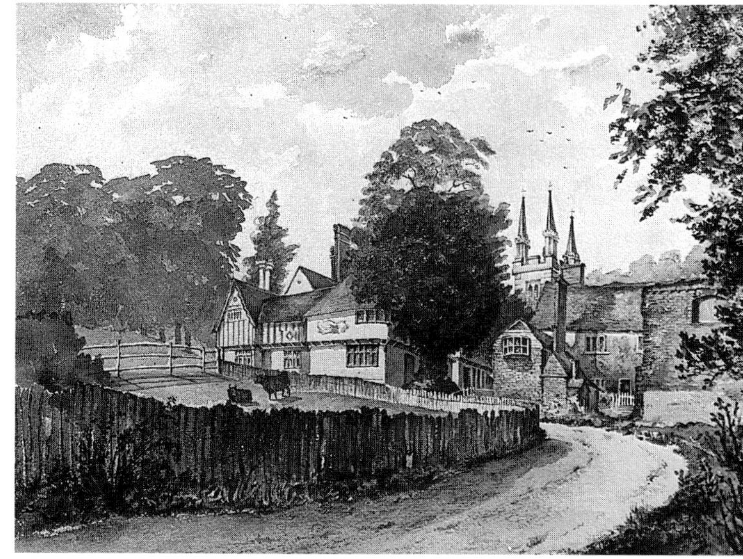

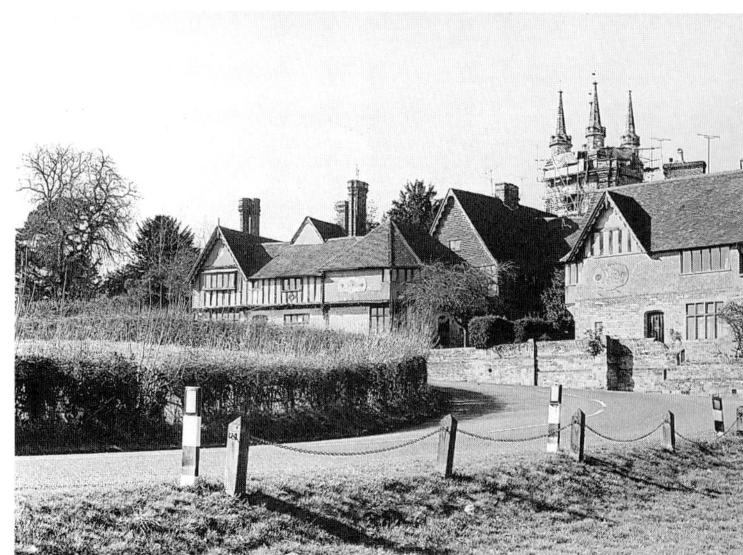

49 *Old cottages at the entrance of ye churchyard, Penshurst, Kent. 1853.*
Compared with recent photograph

42 *Sketch on the Undercliff towards Beachy Head, Mama joined us while sketching, and accompanied us afterwards to the beach under Beachy Head!! tremendous walk for her! 25th Sepr. 1852. L.C.P.*

43 *Taken from Beachy Head Down, Belltout Lighthouse, and the cliffs of Burling* (sic) *Gap in the distance, the last day at Eastbourne, we go to London tommorrow, 30th. Sepr. Wind tremendous,! too high for us to venture near the edge of the cliff. Tom and Rosa joined us here, and we went on to Burling Gap to see the sea, which was magnificent! bitterly cold.*

44 *Burling* (sic) *Gap, Sepr. 30th. 1852. magnificent cliffs further on towards Beachy Head, quite "perpendicular"! Ellen and Muff trying to stand against the gale!* (30)

1853

Suffolk

45 *Bradfield Hall, Suffolk. drove over to sketch it, & the church, with Mr Jeffreys & Miss Latter, July 1853. - L C Paris.*

46 *Sketched from the drawing-room window, Cockfield 1853. L.C.P.*

47 *Sproughton Rectory, from the end of the walk. 1853.* (31)

Kent

48 *Penshurst Castle, Church, and village, from the fields above. 1853.*

49 *Old cottages at the entrance of ye churchyard, Penshurst, Kent. 1853.* (33)

50 *Miss Cresswell's House, Penshurst. Kent, 1853. spent a very pleasant fortnight with her before going to Suffolk, Tom returned from the Mediterranean.*

51 *Part of the Penshurst drawing-room, taken in ten minutes, before I left Miss Cresswell in 1853.* (34)

52 *Penshurst Castle, Kent, sketched in a hurry. Augst. 1853.*

53 *On the Beach between Broadstairs & Kingsgate. 1853.*

54 *Cliffs near Broadstairs, under Mr. Alexander's grounds. 1853.*

55 *Broadstairs Cliffs before a storm, an indefatigable sketcher through storm & sunshine. 1853.*

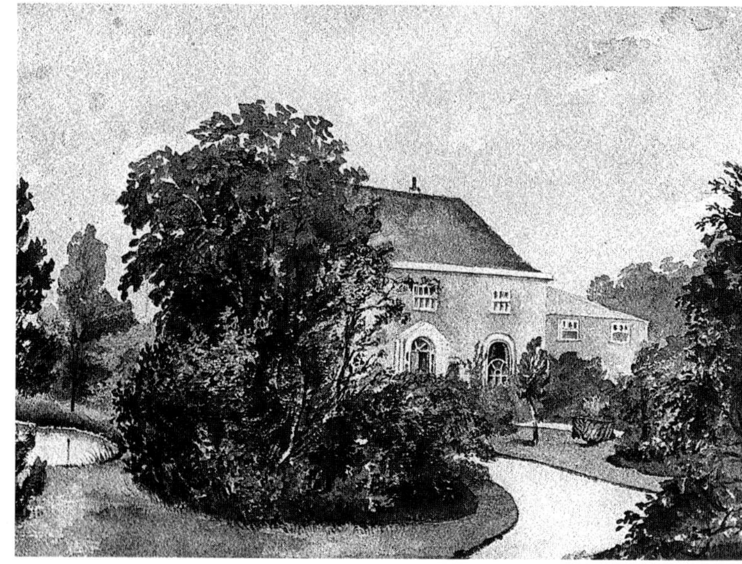

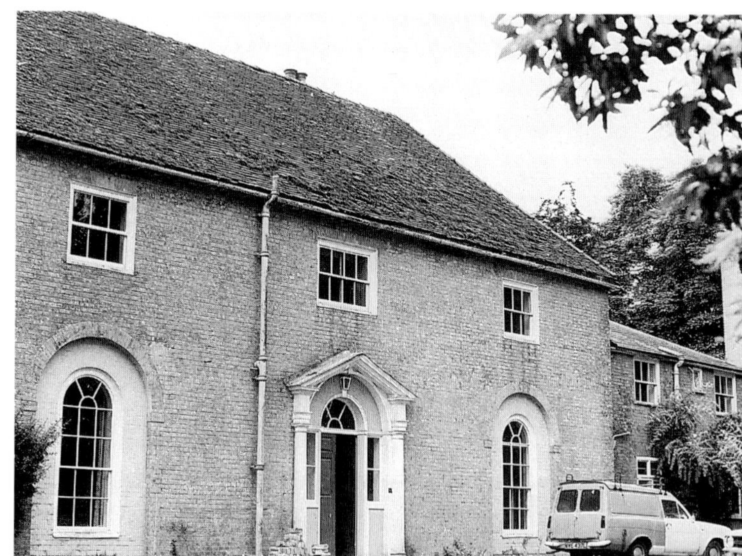

58 *Another view of Cockfield Rectory, taken from the walk near the Moat. 1854.*
Compared with recent photograph

56 Inscribed on reverse: *From the Balcony of Barnes' Library Broadstairs.* (35)
22 x 32.

Surrey

57 *The hotel on Weybridge Common, Surry* (sic), *Mama's cough was so bad I went with her for a week, enjoyed it very much. 1853.*

1854

Suffolk

58 *Another view of Cockfield Rectory, taken from the walk near the Moat. 1854.*

59 *Shrubbery, Cockfield. Mrs. Watson & Miss Latter sketching. 1854.*

60 *Cockfield Church from the second Mill. 1854. L.C.P.*

61 *Cockfield Mill, Mrs. Watson & I sketched it together. 1854.*

62 *Stile in the wood, Cockfield, Lavenham Church in the distance. 1854.*

63 *Sproughton Church, and Mill, 10th. August 1854. I went to stay at Sproughton on the 7th, from Cockfield & left for London on the 12th.* (36)

Kent

64 *Sketch from Saltwood Castle, 22nd. of Septr. walked into the wood afterwards.* (37)

65 *Saltwood, Mama and Fanny came late with Muffy. Tom and Ellen sketched from the top of the wall. Ellen took a likeness of Tom.* (38)

66 *Saltwood Castle from the wood. Mama joined us late in the day. & we all returned together.*

67 *Rosa, Ellen & I walked early to Saltwood & sketched the entrance gate. Mama & Fanny met Miss Kingston & joined us afterwards. beautiful day.* (39)

68 *Entrance to Saltwood Castle, Hythe. I spent the day there with Mama and Fanny. 26th. Sep. 1854. Saltwood Castle is supposed to have been built by the Romans, the sea, it is thought, once washed part of the wood away. now it is more than a mile off. – it was for some years much used by smugglers!*

69 *View from the Downs, Hythe in the valley, the houses, of which we had one, close to the Sea. 27th. Sep. 1854 we spent the day on the Downs.*

70 *Gate at the entrance to the wood, Saltwood, Sep. 28th. Spent the day in sketching. F E & myself. Mama joined us.*

71 *On the road from Saltwood to Sandling Park. Fanny walked with me, leaving Rosa & Ellen sketching at Saltwood. 29th. Sepr.*

72 *Cottage near Sandling Park. Sep. 29th. 1854. Louisa C Paris.*

73 *Going up from Hythe towards Saltwood, walked with Mama to Saltwood afterwards. Sep. 30th. very warm.*

74 *Brockman summer-house at the top of Beechborough Down, near Saltwood. sketched after the dew began to fall.* (40)

75 *A part of Saltwood Castle, spent the day there as usual, more like June than Oct. from the great heat.* (41)

76 *Sketched the day Tom Rosa and myself were left alone, unpleasant day. rained when we reached Saltwood. Octr. 4th. 1854*

77 *Saltwood, 4th. Octr. the day after Mama left Hythe. finished my sketch in the rain. 1854.* (44)

Hampshire

78 *Walhampton, Hants. seat of Sir George Burrard. Bart. Novr. 1854. Mama, Ellen & I spent a fortnight there.*

Note: This has now been re-attributed as Bradfield Hall, Suffolk. An early sketch of Bradfield Hall appears in a recently discovered sketcbook (4). It is identical to the house in this watercolour. The attribution of this building as Walhampton has always been questionable.

79 *The Isle of Wight from Walhampton grounds, - & the Monument to Sir Harry Burrard Neale.*

80 *View of the Needles, from the Mount, Walhampton. Novr. 1854. Louisa Paris.* (45)

81 *View of the Isle of Wight from Walhampton grounds.*
Nov[r]*. 1854. Louisa C. Paris.*

Location and Date Unknown

82 Candle. No inscription or note. (48)
26 x 36.